Primary PE

Primary PE

Unlocking the potential

Anne Williams
Joanne Cliffe

Open University Press

Open University Press
McGraw-Hill Education
McGraw-Hill House
Shoppenhangers Road
Maidenhead
Berkshire
England
SL6 2QL

email: enquiries@openup.co.uk
world wide web: www.openup.co.uk

and Two Penn Plaza, New York, NY 10121-2289, USA

First published 2011

A catalogue record of this book is available from the British Library

ISBN-13: 978–0–33–524233–7 (pb)
ISBN-10: 0–33–524233–2 (pb)
eBook: 978–0–33–524234–4

Library of Congress Cataloging-in-Publication Data
CIP data applied for

Typeset by RefineCatch Limited, Bungay, Suffolk
Printed in the UK by Bell & Bain Ltd, Glasgow

Mixed Sources
Product group from well-managed
forests and other controlled sources
www.fsc.org Cert no. TT-COC-002769
© 1996 Forest Stewardship Council

The *McGraw-Hill* Companies

Contents

Figures

Tables

1   Introduction

Introduction

This book is about helping teachers to make the most of physical education's potential to provide opportunities for enjoyment, achievement and wide-ranging learning. Physical education introduces children to physical activities and skills that can form the foundations for a lifetime of enjoyable and beneficial physical activity, together with the knowledge and understanding to enable them to appreciate the importance of physical activity and the benefits that accrue from regular participation. It also has the potential to contribute to many other curriculum areas – for example, it can reinforce learning in language, mathematics and key cross-curricular topics such as personal, social and health education.

Context

The context for this book is a perceived need for change in the primary curriculum. This perception arises from four areas of policy and research:

- the government-commissioned report on primary education (Rose 2009);
- the need to ensure that primary education engages with the agendas of the *Children's Plan* (DCSF 2007), itself drawing on the priorities set out in *Every Child Matters* (DfES 2003a);
- the need to align the primary curriculum more effectively with a revised secondary curriculum and with the Early Years Foundation Stage (EYFS) so that progression and transition can be improved;
- the need to address growing criticism of the curriculum as overloaded and overprescriptive.

Others, notably the Cambridge Primary Review Group (Alexander 2009), identify further issues including the marginalization of arts and humanities, the distorting effect of national strategies on the curriculum, the loss of breadth and balance between subjects and the adverse effect of Key Stage 2 tests. All of these affect children's experience of physical education, which has been squeezed for time in the primary school and in both initial teacher training and ongoing professional development opportunities. For physical education, the pressures on curriculum time have received some attention through initiatives such as Physical Education and School Sport and Club Links (PESSCL) supported by both the Department for Children Schools and Families (DCSF) and the Department for Culture Media and Sport (DCMS) and promoting the provision of two hours' physical education and sport a week, to include activity both within and beyond the curriculum.

The way in which the primary curriculum is conceptualized and organized has been the focus of two major reviews, the first commissioned by the then DCSF and led by Rose (2009), the second, the Cambridge Primary Review, independent of government, funded by the Esmée Fairbairn Foundation, located at the University of Cambridge and led by Robin Alexander (Alexander 2009). There are some significant differences in their conclusions and recommendations but both envisage the primary curriculum of the immediate future being organized around areas of learning experience that incorporate subjects but that go wider in their ambitions and planned outcomes. Rose recommends that the curriculum be organized into the following areas of experience, designed to progress from Early Learning goals and to map onto the subjects of the secondary curriculum:

- understanding English, communication and language;
- mathematical understanding;
- scientific and technological understanding;
- historical, geographical and social understanding;
- understanding physical development, health and wellbeing;
- understanding the arts (Rose 2009: 31).

The Cambridge Review proposes a slightly different framework, though clearly with very significant overlap:

- arts and creativity;
- citizenship and ethics;
- faith and belief;
- language oracy and literacy;
- mathematics;
- physical and emotional health;
- place and time;
- science and technology (Alexander 2009: 55).

The Cambridge Review deliberately presents the areas of learning alphabetically to avoid the hierarchies explicit in Rose's presentation. This approach chimes with the assertion of David Bell, Her Majesty's Chief Inspector of Schools, in 2004, that 'We cannot afford and our children do not deserve a two-tier curriculum.' The Review also notes that 'The place of subjects in the curriculum remains highly contentious' (Alexander 2009: 4).

A new government has, at the time of writing, yet to make firm decisions about the future form of the primary curriculum but the issues raised above remain relevant. The primary school teacher will continue to need to manage the many competing claims on time whether the curriculum is organized around subjects or areas of experience.

The potential of physical education

The Physical Education and School Sport (PESS) investigation that took place between 2000 and 2007 (PESS 2007) focused on demonstrating the importance of physical education and sport, both within and beyond the curriculum, to the aspirations, wellbeing, attitudes, behaviour and achievements of young people aged from 5 to 16. The examples below show how the project, in many ways, anticipates the challenges of new primary curriculum proposals, providing examples of how physical education contributes beyond the learning of skills, to attainment more broadly, to improving behaviour and to essential skills for learning such as personal and social skills. First, a head teacher describes the impact of physical education and school sport in his school:

Example

Back in 2002 our overall attendance figure of 89 per cent was cause for grave concern and 30 pupils were categorized as 'E' category (close to exclusion). The decision to become involved in the PESS investigation was a lifesaver. I am totally convinced that our commitment to PE and school sport has enabled our children to flourish. We introduced lunch-time activities in zoned play areas and set up new out-of-hours sports clubs . . . We ensured all classes had 2 hours of PE and introduced a new scheme of work . . .

Today attendance stands at 92.9 per cent (it is often as high as 95 per cent) and only two or three pupils occasionally need my (almost) undivided attention at lunchtimes. I would say that this dramatic improvement is largely due to PESS. (PESSCL 2007a)

The next example demonstrates how physical activity goes beyond timetabled lessons and can provide opportunities for children to take responsibility for the learning of others, for taking the lead, working collaboratively and for responding to challenges.

Example

A project to develop pupils' leadership skills and improve behaviour and attitudes to learning

At the start of this investigation, staff at Cherryfield felt that pupils were not being given enough guidance, coordination and support to enable them to make the most of playground activities on offer at lunchtime . . . In the summer of 2006, all Year Four pupils were trained as playground leaders. Additional games were introduced and the young leaders were given hands-on experience of managing and engaging children from reception to Year Six during planning, preparation and assessment (PPA) time. Lunchtime activity this term was based around the football World Cup, a theme that was replicated throughout the school . . .

The play leaders cooperated well with each other, worked effectively and learnt the importance of respect for others. They showed great commitment to the structured activities and rose to the challenge of adapting activities to suit different groups.

Staff were very positive about the impact on pupils and their attitudes towards work in general. (PESSCL 2007a)

The next two examples demonstrate the potential of physical education to improve achievement in other areas while also showing the relevance of physical education to all pupils including those with special needs.

Example

From Hadrian School focusing on improving the handwriting of pupils with severe or profound and multiple learning difficulties by focusing on games activities

Focusing on pupils' handwriting skills at the same time as their games skills paid great dividends. There was a clear link between children's gross and fine motor skills. Pupils' portfolios of work showed an increase in their pace of learning and in the quality of handwriting and hand-eye coordination . . .

Pupils' games skills also improved. Blocking lessons helped them to remember more of what they had learnt and gave them opportunities to practise specific skills more often. They showed a new ability to play simple rule-based games and to work in pairs and small groups. They started to sustain their attention and cooperation throughout a lesson and they became more willing to take turns.

After a term the new Year Four pupils had made significantly more progress than expected in their hand-eye coordination skill and in other PE areas. They were much more confident and independent and staff saw them transferring their skills to other curriculum areas, such as cutting, colouring, handwriting and drawing . . . (PESSCL 2007b)

Example

Using physical education to improve the coordination and concentration of a group of pupils with special educational needs

John was a shy six-and-a-half year old who didn't want to join the gym trail, didn't understand what he was supposed to do and was easily distracted. His coordination was poor and he scored mainly threes, fours and fives on the tests in the original assessment, with one being the highest score and five the lowest. His drawing of a person was assessed as being at the level expected of a child of 3 years and 9 months.

By the end of term, John was scoring one or two on everything except tasks such as doing up buttons and shoelaces. His drawing of a person was assessed as being at the level of a child of 4 years and 9 months – an improvement of a year in one term. (PESSCL 2007b)

These examples demonstrate the potential of physical activity to contribute to a whole range of aspects of learning, development and wellbeing. At the same time they illustrate some of the potential confusion facing the new teacher and the lack of clarity over exactly what is being promoted.

There is explicit reference to the desirability of offering five hours per week of 'physical activity', which includes physical education but also includes some of the activity opportunities shown above, such as the lunchtime and out-of-hours activities in the first example and the playground activities described at Cherryfield in the second. Both demonstrate the significance of physical play and this is also very high profile in the EYFS goals, which emphasize learning through play.

Other case studies of schools demonstrate how the promotion of increased levels of physical activity at lunchtime has led to improvements in behaviour and reductions in exclusions (PESSCL 2007a), part of a range of evidence that involvement in physical education and school sport can improve behaviour and attitudes to learning.

Physical education and learning

The benefits of physical activity are well documented and illustrated by the examples and initiatives described above but it is important to remember that physical education has a place in the curriculum because it makes a particular contribution to learning. Its focus on the physical and on the development of physical capability and competence gives it a unique place within the curriculum.

The outcomes of *High Quality PE and Sport* (DfES 2004) provide a useful summary of what the primary school teacher should be aiming for. High-quality physical education and sport should result in children and young people who:

- are *committed* to physical education and sport and make them a central part of their lives both in and out of school;
- understand that physical education and sport are an important part of a *healthy active lifestyle*;
- have the *confidence* to become involved in physical education and sport;
- have the *skills* and control that they need to take part in physical education and sport;
- willingly take part in a *range of competitive, creative and challenge-type activities*, both as individuals and as part of a team or group;
- *think* about what they are doing and make appropriate *decisions* for themselves;
- *show a desire to improve* and achieve in relation to their own abilities;
- have the *strength, stamina and suppleness* to keep going;
- *enjoy* physical education and school and community sport.

These outcomes bring together a focus on the development of physical competence through learning a range of skills, the development of positive attitudes that lead children to want to participate in physical activity within and beyond school, the development of personal fitness levels necessary for health and the ability to make informed decisions about their performance and participation.

Arnold (1979) identifies three elements to physical education that outline its potential as a learning medium:

- education in movement or in the physical;
- education through movement or through the physical; and
- education about movement or about the physical.

The first takes place through the experience of physical activity. The young child has a keen interest in physical activity and is easily motivated by challenges of a physical nature. Young children enjoy movement for its own sake and delight in mastering physical skills. Education in movement means knowing how to engage in a range of physical activities and involves a belief that such activities are, of themselves, worthwhile and educational. Education in movement has to involve actually taking part in the activities themselves. While there are various activities that are conventionally included within the Early Years or primary curriculum, many different activities could be chosen provided that they enable children to experience and learn. The breadth of learning laid down for physical education includes planning, performing and evaluating in addition to competing and outwitting opponents, creative problem solving, accurate replication of actions and optimum performance. This learning can be achieved through a very wide range of activities. For example, accurate replication may be achieved through the performance of a gymnastics or dance sequence or practising a football skill, but equally through less common curriculum activities such as the repetition of moves in judo or skills in boccia.

Education through movement refers to the use of physical activity as a means of achieving educational ends that are not an intrinsic part of the activity. These encompass cross-curricular aims that are discussed in Chapter 6 and are facilitated in primary settings because children are generally with their class teacher for all subjects. They include using the medium of physical education to achieve learning outcomes in other subject areas. For example, mathematical concepts can be introduced or reinforced in physical education. Language development can be enhanced within the physical education context. Equally significant is the potential of physical education to contribute to other areas of learning such as personal, social and emotional development and personal wellbeing.

Education about movement is key to the achievement of the aims of National Curriculum physical education, which can be summarized as the production of informed and intelligent performers. It is also central to the health focus of primary physical education and to the achievement of the health related outcomes of *Every Child Matters* (DfES 2003a).

These three elements of physical education can be seen in expectations that pupils should take part in physical activities, make links to other areas of learning and learn about healthy lifestyles. Equally, it is clear that achieving the outcomes of high-quality physical education and sport demands education both in (skills and control, participation, strength, stamina and suppleness) and about (understanding, thinking, decision making, healthy lifestyles) the physical. Physical development in the Early Years Foundation Stage also involves all three elements. Young children are expected to be active and improve skills ('education in . . .'), use all of their senses to learn about the world around them ('education through . . .') and develop an understanding of the importance of physical activity ('education about . . .') (DCSF 2008a).

Summary of the book

Chapter 2 discusses physical development, health and wellbeing and the primary school child. It considers knowledge needed by teachers if they are to appreciate the difference between chronological and developmental age and to appreciate the implications of physical development for the child's engagement in physical education, activity or sport. It also addresses how physical education can contribute to a practical understanding of health and to aspects of personal, social and emotional development that enhance wellbeing.

Chapter 3 focuses on learning and teaching styles. It explains key aspects of teaching and learning styles in the context of physical education and provides practical examples and reflective prompts to enable the reader to appreciate the impact of particular teaching strategies on individual pupils. Recent work on approaches to learning, including multiple intelligences, visual, auditory and kinaesthetic learning, which recognize the different ways in which children respond to learning opportunities, will be related to the specifics of the physical education context. While cautioning against extreme approaches that attempt to allow children to work too much within their preferred style, the chapter demonstrates how the use of varied learning and teaching styles can promote effective learning and can contribute to making the curriculum more inclusive.

Chapter 4 focuses on the importance of ensuring that all children have opportunities for success and learning as required by legislation and as an issue related to equity and social justice. The national strategy on inclusion along with the National Curriculum statutory inclusion statement will be used as the basis for consideration of key issues for the classroom teacher. The chapter discusses the meaning of aspects of inclusion in the context of physical education together with potential barriers to attainment related to gender, ethnicity or special educational needs. It will consider key issues such as setting suitable learning challenges, responding to diverse learning needs and overcoming potential barriers to learning and assessment for individuals and groups.

In Chapter 5 the emphasis is on advancing pupil progress and assessment for learning. The different purposes that can be served by assessment will be discussed and related to different methods of assessment. There will be a particular focus on assessment for learning and on how assessment can help the pupil to progress. The principles of assessment for learning as set out by the Assessment Reform Group, such as the promotion of shared learning goals and the development of the capacity for self-assessment, will be applied to specific examples from primary physical education. The relevance of assessment for learning to physical education requirements such as the evaluation and improvement of performance will be stressed and illustrated through case studies. Reflective tasks will be used to focus the reader's attention on appropriate assessment strategies, on feedback to improve performance and on the relationship between strategy, feedback and assessment for learning. Examples will be provided of good assessment practice and how this has the capacity to promote further learning.

Chapter 6 explores cross-curricular opportunities presented by physical education. This chapter will focus on physical education's potential contribution to cross-curricular or linked learning. Its context is a perception that physical education is hard to link with other subjects. At the same time, topic-based approaches, where several subjects contribute to learning key concepts, have begun to reappear in primary schools following the publication of *Excellence and Enjoyment* (DfES 2003b) and have been endorsed by the Rose review's advocacy of high-quality and challenging cross-curricular work (Rose 2009). The chapter will examine what physical education may be able to offer to learning across the primary curriculum, for example to spiritual and moral development, to skills such as thinking, and to topics such as education for sustainable development. It will also discuss how physical education can contribute to learning alongside other subjects, for example applying data-handling skills from mathematics in recording and analysis in athletics, learning about rhythm and pattern in music and dance or working outside the classroom to promote learning in both outdoor and adventurous activities (OAA) and geography local area study.

Chapter 7 discusses creativity. The emphasis will be on teaching for creativity and on developing the creative capabilities of pupils, in line with OfSTED's (2003) finding that the best schools develop creativity in all pupils, irrespective of their ability. The potential of physical education to promote creative environments that encourage outdoor play, exercise, experimentation and managed risk taking, particularly in Early Years education, will be explored, with examples of good practice. Key approaches to developing creativity, such as use of imagination, generation of many responses to a task, experimentation with alternatives, originality of response, elaborating on current knowledge or skill and evaluation of processes and outcomes (Fisher and Williams 2004) will be discussed with specific reference to their use within the physical education context. Examples of innovative practice together with reflective questions and prompts will be used to encourage further critique and development of practice.

Chapter 8 examines the use and abuse of ICT to enhance learning in physical education. The ongoing centrality of ICT, not only as an area of learning in its own right but also as one that should be embedded in the teaching of all subjects, is endorsed strongly by the *Rose Report*. The potential of ICT to contribute to enhancing learning in physical education will be a key focus and some of the pitfalls of misusing ICT will also be highlighted. The chapter will illustrate the effective use of a range of technologies, including camcorders, digital cameras, data recording software (for example spreadsheets), analysis software, the Internet, laptops or palmtops and CD-ROMs or DVDs, through examples of good practice, such as the use of data recording software to log individual performances in athletics or the use of camcorders or digital cameras to analyse and improve dance or gymnastics work.

Chapter 9 looks at the potential of the outdoors to promote learning both in physical education and more widely. The chapter examines how the outdoor classroom can both enhance achievement in physical education and contribute to learning across the curriculum. Its focus will be on the range of outdoor activities that are available to the teacher, both within the school grounds and in the immediate vicinity, and on how these may be used to promote learning. The potential of outdoor learning for subject-related outcomes, for personal and social development, for key skills and for confidence building will be discussed.

Chapter 10 looks at why teachers should become researchers and offers guidance to those starting out to research their own or their school's practice. It discusses the nature of research and its significance for practice, for professional development and for improvements in pupil attainment. Through a focus on action and practitioner research, it will provide practical guidance on planning and completing small-scale school-based projects, taking the reader through the process of developing, refining and implementing individual or small-group projects. It will also address the ethical issues facing the teacher as researcher.

2   Child development and physical education

Introduction

An understanding of the physical development of the primary school child is essential if curriculum planning is to lead to relevant learning experiences for all pupils. As Gallahue (1976: 48) stated, if we are lacking 'a clear understanding of pupils, we become teachers of content rather than teachers of children'. Child development is a complex field of study, covering the biological and psychological changes that occur from birth to adolescence. It is impossible to do justice to all aspects of child development here but it is necessary to consider some of the pertinent changes that transpire during the development of the primary school child. These changes occur as a continuous process, although there are some notable transformations that ensue in stages (often referred to as critical periods of growth) and eventuate as 'milestones'. For example, the process a child goes through when he or she progresses from crawling to walking is a critical stage of early motor development. A thorough understanding of child development helps the primary school teacher to appreciate the range of learning needs within a single classroom and resonates with the entitlements set out in *Every Child Matters* (DfES 2003a).

This chapter focuses on the physical development of the child and will consider the differences between the chronological and developmental ages that a primary school teacher may encounter when faced with the same age pupils in one class. In addition to addressing pupils' physical development, it will also discuss how physical education can contribute to a practical understanding of the nature of pupils' personal and social development. Issues of emotional development and how it can be fostered in a physical education context will be highlighted. Attention will be given to the relationship between child development and possible learning opportunities. This will include examples of matching learning with developmental stages by giving examples of general differences that may be encountered across the Key Stages. The implications for learning of the range of developmental stages within the individual class will be investigated, as will the need to take into account how thinking and planning for the individual child relates to the personalized learning agenda. This chapter will provide examples of physical education scenarios that highlight developmental issues and illustrate how physical education can promote learning. Questions will also be included to prompt the primary school teacher to engage in further reflection and analysis of practice.

Physical development

Most early stages of movement are involuntary using parts or all of the body. A child develops his or her movement reflexively from birth to the Early Years. The primary school teacher needs to be aware of how a child continues to develop his or her movement capabilities. Movements in this context are referred to as gross and fine motor skills, which develop as children grow. Gross motor skills are the large movements that children make by using most of their bodies such as walking, running and jumping. Fine motor skills are smaller movements that are carried out with increasing dexterity, such as progressing from holding a pencil to gripping it in order to draw shapes. The development of these motor skills is noticeable in the first instance from the head to the toes (cephalocaudal) and secondly from the torso to the extremities (proximodistal). Generally, children in the Early Years have control over their movements in their central and upper bodies (gross motor skills) before their lower bodies and extremities of hands and feet, where their dexterity increases later (fine motor skills). Examples of these are given in the reflective activities below:

Reflective activity

Sue wants to observe her Early Years class moving. She is interested to see how their gross motor skills are developing and how the children are able to move using various parts of their bodies. She sets up the learning environment so that the children can engage in unstructured play. She has included the use of padded mats and padded blocks of various shapes and sizes. Sue observes her pupils crawling, walking, rolling over, running and jumping. Sue notices that two children appear to be 'clumsy' and not as physically able as their peers.

- What aspects of development are the two children displaying?
- How can Sue aid their physical development?

Reflective activity

Sue works with her Early Years class on throwing and catching activities. She provides the children with various implements to throw, including balls, bean bags, quoits and a variety of 'alternative' balls. Some children are able to throw and catch with ease, others are finding the activities challenging and are having difficulties gripping some of the equipment.

- What might be the reasons for the differences in the children's abilities?
- How can Sue address the learning needs of all the pupils in the class?

It is important to remember that physical development is a process, and as children progress to Key Stage 1 and through to Key Stage 2 their motor skills develop as they continue to grow and are exposed to effective teaching and learning. However, the teacher can expect pupils to develop at different rates. There will be variation within one class in terms of height, weight, muscular strength, flexibility and stamina. Such variation poses a challenge for the teacher in terms of meeting pupils' individual needs. A teacher must also take into consideration pupils' development of eye-limb coordination, reaction time and whole-body coordination to articulate movement. The physical development of children can be observed during their play, as the following example illustrates.

Reflective activity

The Early Years movement class is working on travelling with its teacher, David. David notices that most of the children can walk in a straight line and can hop on each foot. In observing the class, he can see that some children are demonstrating more control over their movements than others. Those demonstrating more control are showing bodily coordination and strength in their hopping and they can also balance reasonably well on one foot. Those who are working with less control appear to be moving slowly and lacking in whole body strength. They are also struggling to hold their balance and, as they land, they flail their arms.

- What are the reasons for the differences in the children's performance?
- How can David's teaching make a difference to the children's performance?

Most early patterns of movement progression in children are noticeable to the primary school teacher. However, it is helpful to know more precisely what movements children are capable of at the different stages of their primary schooling. Drawing on somewhat limited research on motor development, Gallahue and Ozmun (1998) presented a theoretical model of motor development to chart children's movement behaviour. By the time children reach the end of the Early Years of schooling, they are capable of demonstrating movement abilities including balance, travel and manipulation activities (such as throwing and catching a ball).

Fundamental movement phase (initial, elementary and mature stages)

The developmental period from the Early Years to the end of Key Stage 1 is referred to as the fundamental movement phase according to Gallahue and Ozmun's (1998) model and is divided into three stages: initial, elementary and mature. The initial phase of fundamental movement covers children's development most seen in the Early Years. Although they are capable of a limited range of movement, children will be developing their coordination as it is common to see younger children with a very poor repertoire of movement. The elementary phase of movement sees children develop greater coordination and rhythmical flow as they move into Key Stage 1. Although there is obviously overlap between all the stages, when children reach the mature stage, they start to produce movements of more control and precision. For example, pupils are capable of producing sequences in gymnastics that show poise and appropriate body tension. At this stage, some children are more than capable of completing sophisticated movements that rely on visual-motor requirements. These movements often involve manipulation whilst on the move, such as catching or striking a moving ball. However, it may well be the case that children do not develop these types of movement until they are in Key Stage 2 (or beyond) as aspects of these movements rely on acquisition of skills and are best taught.

Specialized movement phase (transitional and application stages)

The specialized movement phase follows the fundamental movement phase and commences with the transitional stage. The transitional stage builds on what went before and movement becomes even more controlled and elaborate. For example, this could be the difference between a child swimming 'doggy paddle' to swimming a recognized stroke with greater technical efficiency. It is during this phase, generally in Key Stage 2, that children can demonstrate competence in a number of activities (this can drop off by Key Stage 3) and they are also very keen to learn. This stage of a child's development is often known as the 'skill-hungry years' (Williams 1996a; Kirk 2005) and provides the opportunity for the primary school teacher to capture children's interest and enthusiasm. Gallahue and Ozmun (1998) describe this period of child development as exciting.

There will be some children whose talent sees them into the next stage of application in the specialized movement phase. A child who has reached this level whilst still at primary school demonstrates the ability to make and implement decisions, such as applying tactics in a game situation. On the other hand, at this stage, some children try to avoid involvement in some or all activities due to the emphasis on skill and accuracy of movement. Therefore, consideration should be given to other aspects of child development and to the learning environment.

Personal and social development

Personal and social development have been considered important aspects of the primary curriculum for some time and both aspects are embedded in physical education teaching. Rose (2009) promotes the idea that primary schools should capitalize on the wealth of opportunities available to them but should also recognize the challenges that a focus on personal and social development brings. Physical education can foster positive links to the teaching of personal, social and health education. In particular, all issues of inclusion (see Chapter 4) including how to respect others and how to be aware of equal opportunities should be addressed in teaching and learning. Working with others, involving listening to and respecting ideas, can be incorporated in different physical education contexts, from creative problem-solving activities to cooperation and fairness in games. Rose (2009) gives the example that to develop self-belief children should develop their leadership skills and be given the opportunities to take the lead. Physical education lends itself to many leadership opportunities for children.

Reflective activity

Year Three is working on a module of tag rugby, whilst the pupils are learning new skills. Alan is keen for them to understand fair play and have respect for others. Alan finds that the pupils are quick to play by the rules he introduces and now he wants the children to take more responsibility. He sets the children a task of organizing a mini tournament and encourages the children to share out the roles of playing and officiating and to take turns. Alan gives the children the opportunity to pick their own teams but there is one child no one wants to pick.

- How should Alan intervene to resolve this situation?
- In what alternative ways could Alan have approached this lesson?

Example

The outdoor and adventurous activity lesson for Year Six is being taught by Sheena. Sheena has been focusing on orienteering and she aims to give the pupils the opportunity to work with others with a focus on leadership. Sheena selects the pupils who are to be leaders of small groups and she briefs them as to what she is expecting them to do with their teams. The children complete the orienteering tasks and Sheena asks the pupils questions in order to evaluate their performance, both as a team and, in particular, how the children felt about leading and their responsibilities.

It should be remembered that children enter primary schools from a variety of different backgrounds including those from broken families, those that are impoverished and those who have English as an additional language. Some children have very poor social skills and language difficulties (DCSF 2008b; Alexander 2009). This can lead to negative effects on children's learning and wellbeing, and this poses challenges for teachers when dealing with the implications of variations in an individual's development. Further links to personal, social and health education can be made as children need to learn to value each other irrespective of their social backgrounds or physical abilities (DfEE/QCA 1999).

Example

Jane teaches physical education to all year groups. She has a good understanding of what the children are capable of in terms of their physical, personal and social development. For her Year One games class, working on ball skills, she expects the children to be able to perform basic underarm throws with a variety of equipment including balls and bean bags, and most pupils can do this. Some pupils will be able to use more technical skills when throwing, including performing overarm throws. Some of the pupils can devise throwing games and can explain these to others. However, there are some who are struggling to make progress and they find it difficult to work as team members.

In the Year Six class, most pupils are able to use a variety of techniques and show consistency in passing and receiving a ball. Most understand the rules of the ball games they play and can work as members of a team by organizing themselves. Most are able to recognize strengths and weaknesses of their own and others' play. Some children will work with quality and select and apply appropriate tactics in game situations. However, there are some children who are struggling with most aspects of the lesson. In particular, they use a limited range of throws and are lacking in willingness to offer ideas and to share these with the class.

These two classes illustrate that there are differences in what pupils are able to do in a given year group. Even though the Year Six pupils are mostly able to engage in more cooperative work than Year One, both age ranges may have children who have poorly developed social skills.

Emotional development

Many aspects of personal and particularly social development overlap with emotional development, which is gaining prominence in all aspects of education. Often, emotion and the development of emotion are referred to in the same context as emotional intelligence, however they are not the same thing (Cliffe 2008). Considerable scientific research into aspects of intelligence led to the coining of the term 'emotional intelligence' by Salovey and Mayer (1990: 189). They describe it as 'a type of social intelligence that involves the ability to monitor one's own and others' emotions, to discriminate among them, and to use the information to guide one's thinking and actions'. The concept was popularized in the late 1990s with Goleman (1995: 43) being given credit for its success. Goleman described emotional intelligence in terms of 'knowing one's emotions . . . managing emotions . . . motivating oneself. . . . recognising emotions in others . . . [and] handling relationships'. In essence, emotional intelligence is someone's ability to make intelligent use of their own or others' emotions and this develops over time and with life experience (Cliffe 2008, 2011).

Teachers ought to be mindful that there are a vast number of commercial packages that, despite the lack of empirical research, claim to measure and enhance children's emotional intelligence. These should perhaps be approached with caution, particularly with regard to resources originating from the US, which by their very nature are fraught with cultural differences and nuances of language (Cliffe 2008). Some schools have embraced the Social and Emotional Aspects of Learning programme (known as SEAL), which was developed by the National Strategies as part of the behaviour and attendance strategy (Alexander 2009; Rose 2009). Many of the resources associated with this programme are being used to address emotion in discrete lessons. Alexander (2009) advises against these discrete lessons, pointing out that what is being taught is not a subject but 'a state of mind'. He recommends that it be considered in the same way as 'wellbeing' and that all aspects of teaching and learning contribute to its development. Therefore, the primary school teacher ought to be addressing the emotional development of children where appropriate in all teaching and learning and in this context, as it is related to the thinking and feeling associated with active involvement in physical education.

Example

In athletics Laura is working on running technique with her Year Six class. The pupils are refining their sprinting technique and have responded well to drills which have helped them to develop their style. Laura tells the class that they are going to race and be timed. Some pupils are excited by this prospect but some are horrified at the thought of being compared to others and coming last. Laura uses this opportunity to encourage the pupils to share what they are thinking and feeling.

There may be 'general' personal, social and emotional issues that primary school teachers have to deal with on a day-to-day basis, such as differences in pupils' home backgrounds, as already mentioned, but being aware of pupils' emotional issues in physical education assists teachers in maximizing the children's learning opportunities. Emotions and feelings that are inextricably linked are experienced in different ways by different children. Teachers may need to deal sensitively with social and emotional issues such as friendship groups when doing partner or group work, especially as empathy develops over time, although it can be improved with teacher intervention.

Example

Year Four is engaging in partner work in gymnastics, creating sequences that include body shape, balance and travel. Although they are used to working in pairs, there are friendship groups in the class who react negatively to being split up. Nicky lets the pupils decide who they will partner. There is one couple left who have not worked together before and who do not want to now. They misbehave by being off-task and distracting others. Nicky takes the opportunity to discuss how members of the class are feeling. By encouraging the pupils to talk about their emotions, she promotes the need to value others and accept that other pupils' feelings are important.

Example

Pupils in Year Four are going swimming for the first time. Whilst some pupils are looking forward to their lessons, there are others who feel fearful. Vanessa knows that pupils who are afraid are less likely to take risks or try new experiences which often results in a loss of confidence in their ability to make decisions. Vanessa incorporates the use of 'circle time' to encourage the pupils to talk about their fears. Vanessa makes links with stories in English in her efforts to reassure the children.

Example

Lesley is taking her Year Five pupils on an outdoor and adventurous activity residential experience. For some children, this is the first time they have been away from their homes. Lesley works with the children on a number of cross-curricular activities to make the proposed trip less daunting. In particular, Lesley uses adventure stories in English and she encourages the pupils to express what they are thinking and feeling. In the trusting environment she has established the pupils are able to be honest about their feelings and this helps to ease their fears.

It is possible to make literacy connections when promoting aspects of personal, social and emotional development. Dealing with these elements of the curriculum can enable teachers to develop pupils' emotional literacy. Through physical education children can learn approaches to express their emotions as they cooperate and listen to others. Steiner and Perry (1997: 11) claim emotional literacy is composed of three abilities: 'the ability to understand your emotions, the ability to listen to others and empathize with their emotions, and the ability to express emotions productively'.

This approach can also aid a child's initial understanding of physical intelligence. Physical intelligence is closely aligned to motor skills and has traditionally been thought of in terms of dance (Carter 1998). Physical intelligence develops over time and encompasses the embodiment of an individual. It also draws on aspects of motivation, confidence, knowledge and understanding of physical competence. There are obviously feelings and emotions associated with physical competence; therefore it would aid children's learning if they were able to articulate how and what movement feels like.

Planning for learning

The child's physical and psychological development is due to both genetic and environmental factors. This is worth considering when planning for learning. One view is that thinking and learning occur as a natural process with teachers matching learning tasks to the stage the child has reached; another view is that it is the teacher's job to develop children by moving them beyond their current state. Alexander (2009: 95) illustrates the latter approach with Vygotsky's (1978: 89) maxim that 'the only good teaching is that which outpaces development'. In terms of the physical development of a child, the context here is that an understanding of child development can help the teacher to maximize pupils' learning.

In planning for learning that promotes different aspects of development, it is beneficial to consider how teaching styles (see Chapter 3) affect learning. Mosston and Ashworth (2002) claim that there are development opportunities in every lesson. For example, planning for decision making or responding to questions mean the pupils are invited to think (using cognitive processes) whilst being active (engaging in the physical processes) and working with others (social process) while respecting the rules (ethical process) and demonstrating their self-control (emotional process). The primary school teacher thus has a unique opportunity to view cognitive processes in action as children demonstrate their thinking whilst moving.

Learning that impacts on physical, personal, social and emotional development is significant in the overall development of the primary school child. This is highlighted by Alexander (2009) who refers to the importance of these aspects of development but stresses that they should not be regarded as added on to physical education – more that aspects of development (including health) be properly understood and integrated into the subject.

Rose (2009) reported that there need to be appropriate and innovative ways of assessing pupils' progress in the physical, personal, social and emotional development areas. However, teaching that is planned to maximize children's learning is likely to incorporate assessment for learning strategies (see Chapter 5). For example, a pupil can experience good feelings of success during constructive feedback. A teacher can assist the pupil's understanding by providing concrete information about their performance. The interplay of cognitive, physical and emotional processes can enhance a child's thinking process and subsequent performance.

Implications for teaching approaches and the importance of play

The aim of this chapter has been to provide an understanding of children's development and ways in which primary school teachers can address the learning needs of the pupils in their physical education lessons. Whilst seeking to provide meaningful measures to assist teachers in their thinking and planning for learning, it has raised some issues regarding difficulties that teachers may encounter. However, one of the biggest challenges for the teacher is coping with the variation in developmental levels in the single class. Reference has been made to how children grow and develop, and the issues teachers ought to consider when meeting these needs have been noted. However, teachers are also faced with implications posed by different rates of maturation, which highlight differences between the chronological and developmental ages of children.

In addition to issues regarding school starting ages and the effects these have on children's development (those who are 'young' summer births or those who are 'old' autumn births), children vary in their rates of development. Individual physical differences in a 'typical' class are usually noticeable and can be as much as five developmental years (Williams 1996a). The progressive phases and associated stages of motor development have been outlined but children do not fit neatly into such categories. It is best that these phases are viewed as a sliding scale and a teacher does need to be wary that, although children are grouped according to their chronological age, there will be differences in their rates of maturation. A teacher will need to differentiate activities skilfully to ensure that all remain motivated to learn. This can be achieved by setting different tasks, using modified equipment or in grouping. For example, if children are engaged in counter balance activities in gymnastics, they should be matched according to their size.

Reflective activity

Mary's Year Six class is playing rounders. The pupils know and understand the rules and have a good knowledge of positioning. Mary is comparing the physical development of the pupils in the class. Not all the children are confident to play with a rounders ball, so Mary is letting them use a tennis ball; however, Mary notices that two pupils who are fielding are missing catches. The children run to the ball with their arms outstretched but cannot complete the catches, although when practising static throwing and catching they did demonstrate some success.

- What reasons could there be for difficulties in catching the ball?
- How can Mary address the learning needs of these pupils?

Overall, teachers need to accept the challenges they face in order to maximize children's learning potential. A greater understanding of child development and learning allows good planning which brings about effective teaching of physical education.

Whilst movement is central to a child's play, the child learns to move by being engaged in physical activity, hence children move to learn and learn to move. Play is essential in the Early Years as children are naturally curious about their surroundings. Therefore, it is beneficial to create an environment which provides opportunities for playful exploration in order to nurture a child's growth and development. Indeed, the physical educational process for many is rooted in Arnold's (1979) three dimensions of education *in*, *through* and *about* movement (Kirk 1988; Williams 1989; Kirk et al. 1996) (see Chapter 1). These dimensions are applicable to physical education in the primary school. The process of moving is at the heart of 'education in movement' which assists the choices made which lead to worthwhile intrinsic activities. Children enjoy moving in physical experiences, particularly when they learn new skills or are involved in imaginative performances where they feel a sense of success. Learning in movement can be associated with the stages in the fundamental movement phase.

Extrinsic outcomes such as moral and social values are consequences of 'education through movement'. Teachers can provide a host of learning experiences through movement; this could be for the sake of engaging in a particular activity, cross-curricular work or in developing aspects of personal, social and emotional development. For example, through OAA, children can learn about how they feel and how they should address their feelings when participating in activities which could be outside their 'comfort zone'.

'Education about movement' aids the children's ability to think in physical terms, thus contributing to their cognitive development. This aspect of learning comes to the fore in the specialized movement phase. Education about movement is where children enhance their knowledge and develop their understanding, although it is possible that they are able to grasp physical concepts but are unable to demonstrate them physically. Overall, exercise is a consequence and benefit of physical movement and play, whether in, through or about movement. Activity contributes to the process of child development.

The importance of personalized learning

Having outlined aspects of physical, personal, social and emotional development that affect a child's wellbeing, it is important for a teacher to know how to address personalized learning for each child, which should also be linked to inclusion and meeting individual needs (see Chapter 4). As a starting point, teachers should distinguish a child's strengths and be able to identify areas for development. Children can be taught to recognize how they learn best and how to approach aspects of their learning that they may find difficult. Early encouragement from the teacher for children to take responsibility for their own learning helps to foster a work ethic where children develop commitment to self-improvement through determination and by showing initiative. Realizing and identifying their own achievements helps children to become aware of what is possible, which aids their self-confidence. It also develops their ability to respond and deal with praise and constructive criticism (Rose 2009).

Example

Tim is responsible for teaching all aspects of the primary curriculum to his Year Three class. He addresses individual needs by differentiating his teaching, but Tim realizes that if he knows his pupils well he can provide more meaningful differentiation to personalize their individual learning. In planning, Tim considers the children individually and works to match his teaching to his pupils' needs. Initially Tim considers that this teaching approach is time-demanding as he has a large class. In reality, Tim finds that considering his pupils as individuals, lesson by lesson, helps him to become more attuned to their needs and raises his expectations of what they can achieve.

Rose (2009) recommends that children set and work towards personal development targets by reflecting on their past achievements and experiences, and that children should learn to manage their future learning and behaviour. In addition, children should be encouraged to work independently and be aware of when they should seek help. Setting the scene for personalized learning can be demanding in terms of a teacher's planning and organization and may require far more input in Early Years and Key Stage 1. It is important that teachers build in assessment opportunities, particularly when addressing pupils' personal targets.

Aspects of emotional wellbeing can be brought into personalized learning of physical education. Whilst pupils are taught and encouraged to explore their range of movement, drawing on skills, knowledge and understanding, they can be encouraged to develop an awareness of their own and others' feelings.

Summary

This chapter has highlighted the difference between chronological and developmental age and how the primary or Early Years teacher needs to plan for wide-ranging differences within a single class. It has also drawn attention to aspects of personal, social and emotional development of relevance to the teacher who wishes to maximize learning. The need to use a range of teaching approaches and to personalize learning was emphasized.

3   Learning and teaching styles

Introduction

A practical understanding of learning and teaching styles is important if the full potential of physical education is to be unlocked. The breadth of learning outcomes that may be achieved in and through physical education is illustrated by:

- the position statement issued by the UK physical education profession in 2005, which points to both the learning of a range of skills and techniques and to the provision of a context for a wide range of learning related to many different dimensions of education, including across the curriculum (see Chapter 6 for further material on physical education and cross-curricular learning), and to other themes including personal and social development;
- the current National Curriculum physical education programme of study, which includes not only the acquisition and development of skills but also the selection and application of those skills, evaluating and improving performance and knowing and understanding about fitness and health;
- the current National Curriculum general physical education requirements, which include contributing to language across the curriculum, to the development of ICT capability, to spiritual, moral, social and cultural development, to key skills such as communication and application of number and to understanding of health and safety (QCDA 1999);
- the *Every Child Matters* (DfES 2003a) agenda, which includes health, safety, enjoyment and achievement, positive contributions to society and economic wellbeing, with clear implications for physical education and how it is taught and learned.

However, both QCA (2005a) and OfSTED (2005) point to a tendency towards too much teacher domination and focus on management and organization and a lack of active pupil involvement in learning in primary physical education. These, they say, lead to weaknesses in understanding and decision making even though pupils can demonstrate skills and involvement in healthy activity. They are also inconsistent with the pupil learning preferences reported by the QCA in 2007, that included learning in active ways, being involved rather than listening for too long, lessons involving discussion, debate and practical activities, paired or group work and activities where they feel challenged (QCDA 2008: 7).

The significance of different learning and teaching styles thus depends in part on teachers who wish to use the full potential of physical education as a learning medium. While the practical nature of physical education is likely to favour the kinaesthetic learner, using a variety of teaching styles can promote a much wider range of learning outcomes and provide learning experiences that are enjoyable and successful for a far wider range of learning styles and preferences.

This is not to say that pupils either could or should be allowed to use their preferred style all the time, even if this were practicable. The styles are preferences rather than requirements and, to succeed later in life, pupils will need to be able to learn in different ways and to adapt to different learning contexts and circumstances. However, it is clear that if the full range of subject learning outcomes is to be achieved, cross-curricular potential is to be exploited and the *Every Child Matters* agenda is to be addressed successfully, both learning and teaching styles need to be varied.

This chapter will help the teacher to enhance learning and achievement in physical education through a better understanding of learning and teaching styles and the relationship between them and how pupils learn. It will begin with a reminder of the nature of learning in physical education that will set the context for the remainder of the chapter. Learning styles will be examined and related to specific physical education examples. Teaching styles will be reviewed and related to the kinds of learning that different styles may promote. Throughout, examples and reflective activities will illustrate how individual pupils respond to different teaching and learning approaches.

Learning styles and learning preferences

There have been many different categorizations of learning style over recent years. In looking to see how these might be viewed in a manageable way by the teacher for the purposes of this book, it is useful to subdivide an individual's learning style into:

- how learners prefer to receive information (visual, auditory, kinaesthetic);
- how individuals choose to process information (sequential, random); and
- different ways of being intelligent (linguistic, logical/mathematical, spatial, bodily-kinaesthetic, musical, interpersonal, intrapersonal, naturalistic) (Hughes 2002).

Visual, auditory and kinaesthetic learners

Visual learners tend to learn through watching. They like information that is presented visually. They will enjoy working from pictures and posters and from short video clips of physical activities and skills. As some like text and some appreciate pictures and diagrams, work cards and sheets that include both pictures and text will accommodate the needs of these learners effectively. Demonstrations will be an effective teaching technique for these pupils.

Auditory learners prefer listening. They will appreciate verbal explanations, discussing their work and listening to instructions. They like to hear information. For these pupils, the commentary that accompanies a demonstration, or the discussion that follows it, will be as important as the demonstration itself.

Kinaesthetic learners like to learn by doing. They enjoy physical activity and may well be the pupils who fidget through task setting or demonstrations as they just want to get on with practising.

Reflective activity

Jane is teaching gymnastics to Year Five. Each child is working on matching balances and actions with a partner. Jane has provided the class with task cards showing pictures of various balances and written tasks, including copying the balance on the sheet or finding a more challenging alternative and making it easier. Jane asks Kim and Mark to demonstrate their three chosen balances to the rest of the class, who are asked to watch and then choose one to try themselves. While they watch, the children are asked to describe the good points of the demonstration and to discuss, with their partners, how to achieve the same level of performance. Members of the class suggest good body tension, watching your partner carefully then copying and choosing carefully to make sure that both can perform the chosen balance.

- In what ways do the above accommodate different styles of learning?

The class continues the work in the following lesson. Jane uses the same task cards and has also put some photographs of work from the previous school year on the wall. This time, rather than a whole-class demonstration, Jane asks one pair to show their work and invites the rest of the class either to come and watch or to continue practising if they would prefer to do that. She asks a second pair to show their work and to describe how they have chosen their balances and what they have done to improve them.

- How have different learning styles been accommodated further in this lesson?
- What questions might Jane pose to extend the pupils' learning beyond the physical skills involved?

Reflective activity

Mark is introducing a dance activity based on the pyramids that link to learning from a class topic on the Egyptians. He shows the Year Three pupils pictures from ancient Egypt and plays music that he feels will suggest appropriate actions and dynamics. The pupils talk enthusiastically about possible dance ideas. The teacher gives two directions – make strong shapes based on the structure of pyramids and improvise actions and movement to show pyramids being built. He tells the class that its dances will be videoed once completed. The teacher constantly asks questions to encourage pupils to reflect on what they are doing. He also gives them frequent opportunities to watch and comment on each other's work particularly where he sees something unusual or innovative. The pupils also ask each other questions such as 'What if we do this?' 'How about trying it that way?'

- What kinds of learners will benefit from Mark's approach and how?

(This case study is based on a QCA example, see www.qcda.gov.uk.)

Sequential and random processing of information

Some individuals choose to process information in a logical and sequential manner and will not be comfortable with tasks or lessons that lack structure. Others approach information in a more random and intuitive way and will tend to find sequential carefully ordered approaches irritating and restrictive. Sequential learners may find very open-ended tasks frustrating while random processors will thrive on the freedom that this approach provides.

Reflective activity

Deepak is teaching ball skills to Year Four. He asks the class to experiment with different ways of throwing and catching and work out what works best if you want to get the ball to travel a long distance. Some groups continue to work at the task for some time, trying out one- and two-handed throws and both overarm and underarm techniques, although not everyone in each group is equally involved. A couple of groups stop working after a very short time and when Deepak asks them to keep going, they complain that they are bored and ask why he doesn't show them the best ways and how to go about improving.

- What kinds of learners are best suited to this task? How could Deepak adapt it so that all were motivated to continue?

Different kinds of intelligence

Howard Gardner's work on multiple intelligences dates from 1983 and suggests that intelligence, rather than being one-dimensional and fixed, is multi-dimensional. Individuals have a range of intelligences, possessing each to some degree. The nine he proposes are:

- Linguistic – the ability to learn and use language.
- Logical/mathematical – the capacity to analyse problems logically and carry out mathematical operations.
- Musical – skills in the performance, composition and appreciation of musical patterns.
- Spatial/visual – facility with images and the ability to recognize and manipulate patterns.
- Kinaesthetic – the ability to use the body and to enjoy activities that involve movement, dance, sport or other physical activities.
- Interpersonal – the ability to communicate with and work with other people.
- Intrapersonal – the capacity to know oneself and to be self-motivated.
- Naturalistic – enjoyment of the natural world.
- Existential – facility to question life, death and ultimate realities (Gardner 1999).

The balance within any individual has an important influence on the way in which that person will learn. For example, the interpersonal learner will thrive on group work and discussion while the intrapersonal learner is likely to be more comfortable working independently. This has implications not only for teaching approaches within physical education lessons but for the activities that are chosen to make up the individual school or class physical education curriculum.

Reflective activity

Whitechapel Primary School has chosen to teach Year Five physical education using a sport education model in which pupils are put into learning groups or teams within which they all take on a variety of assigned roles. Pupils work in these groups for each unit of work. They gain experience as performers, recorders and coaches irrespective of activity and, where appropriate, as referees.

Malden Junior School has decided to include invasion games and racket games in its curriculum for Year Five together with gymnastics in the winter and athletics in the summer. Pupils work in groups to create their own games in the invasion games lessons and in pairs for the racket games lessons. There is a strong focus on cooperative play in the racket games lessons. In gymnastics there is a mix of individual compositional work and partner and group work leading to both individual and group sequences performed for assessment by other members of the class. Athletics lessons are based on personal target setting and on working to improve on their previous best.

- Which of the above will best meet the need of both intra and interpersonal learners?
- What potential is there for learning through multiple intelligences?
- What adaptations would broaden the curriculum's appeal to all learners?

Planning for multiple intelligences is linked to planning for learning through movement as well as about movement. While physical education can clearly relate to kinaesthetic intelligence, there is enormous potential for planning to encompass other intelligences also, thus broadening its appeal and widening the potential for all to achieve. Some of this planning overlaps with that aiming to accommodate different approaches to receiving and processing information.

Reflective activity

Dawn is teaching gymnastics to Year Five. She uses work cards with both pictures and words to set the class a task of creating sequences that include linking movements, changes of speed and direction. The class is split into groups of four or five and they have to work within their group with a shared approach to some options about which they have to make decisions. Options given to the class include working to music, played while they work, working to a common floor pattern that they have to design, or planning a sequence of matching actions performed simultaneously. One member of each group is to introduce the performance to the rest of the class, describing the content of the sequence, the options selected and the challenges faced in its planning and practising.

- How would the above promote the use of multiple intelligences within the class and within each group?
- Look again at the example of Jane's teaching on p. 27. What intelligences does Jane's approach utilize?
- How might she adapt her approach to maximize the opportunities for pupils to use logical/mathematical intelligence or interpersonal intelligence?

The more balanced the curriculum is across the National Curriculum activity areas, the greater the opportunity for pupils to use multiple intelligences in their learning. For example, dance can engage pupils' musical, linguistic and spatial intelligence in addition to the obvious kinaesthetic intelligence, maybe through the use of musical and verbal stimuli or the development of floor and air patterns. Team games require the use of interpersonal intelligence whereas athletics or swimming may give opportunities for individual and self-motivated learning, although this will, of course, depend on the teaching styles and approaches chosen.

Compositional work in both dance and gymnastics can use visual/ spatial intelligence. Logical/mathematical intelligence may be used in the analysis of fitness data collected as part of teaching about health and fitness, linking with data handling in mathematics, and in using gymnastics or dance to reinforce work in mathematics. This could include teaching concepts such as reflective symmetry or quarter, half and full turns at Key Stage 1.

Reflective activity

Asheefa is teaching Year Five games. She has split the class into groups of eight, each of which has created a small side invasion game in a designated space, with limited choice of equipment (different kinds of goals, various sizes and types of balls). Two groups are playing 4 v 4, with a goal scored by bouncing a large ball into a hoop. An argument is beginning in both groups because nobody has scored and the game has been going on for some time. Asheefa draws the pupils' attention to the guidance on a laminated sheet available to each group that suggests different ways of making points scoring easier – changing the size of the playing space or the goal; changing the equipment (the ball); changing the numbers on each team; and changing the scoring method – and she involves both groups in a discussion of how to improve matters. One group decides to play 5 v 3 and the other to use a bench on which the ball has to be touched rather than the hoop. Goals are then scored in both games.

- How does this lesson enable pupils to use multiple intelligences?
- What kinds of learners and intelligences might be less successful?

Reflective activity

James is teaching swimming to Year Three using the local pool for a 5-week block. Prior to their first visit to the pool, James worked with the class and they produced posters about safety – these are displayed in the classroom and on the poolside. They have also watched a short DVD of pupils the same age learning to swim and have discussed how well these pupils have swum and the difficulties faced by some of them. James made laminated cards with pictures and verbal descriptions of different ways in which the pupils can propel themselves through the water. These are available on the poolside for reference throughout the lesson. The pupils are also keeping swimming diaries that give a record of what they have learned and also of the water-based activities undertaken each week. At the end of the swimming unit they use these to produce bar charts and pie charts showing the proportions of the class succeeding in various water-based tasks.

- How has James enabled pupils to use multiple intelligences during this block work?
- How far is he enabling visual, auditory and kinaesthetic learners to use their preferred learning styles?
- What opportunities are there for cross-curricular learning (see Chapter 6)?

In order to enable pupils to have opportunities to use a range of learning styles, the teacher needs to be familiar with a range of teaching styles and strategies. Teaching styles, in the context of physical education, have tended to be categorized on a continuum with closed, wholly teacher-directed approaches at one extreme and very open-ended approaches at the other. Another way of describing them is to determine the extent to which approaches are teacher or student-mediated (Siedentop and Tannehill 2000) – that is, how much responsibility the pupils are given. Mosston and Ashworth's (2002) work on teaching styles links style with progress in various aspects of development that might be relevant to the physical education teacher. Some of them are outlined below:

- Command style – the teacher is dominant and makes all the decisions. The pupil's role is to try to attain the standards of performance demanded by the teacher. This style produces uniformity, conformity, quick response to instructions and adherence to a specific performance model demonstrated by the teacher. For example, the teacher demonstrates a shoulder balance to Year Three for the whole class to copy.
- Practice style – while the teacher still dictates the activity, the pupils practise in their own time. For example, the teacher asks a pupil to demonstrate the forehand drive in short tennis, pointing out key teaching points such as the stance, the preparation for the stroke, timing, and the follow-through. The whole class then practises the shot in their own time, dropping the ball and hitting into the fencing around the playing area.
- Inclusion style – here the teacher sets a task within which there are options so that pupils can select the one most appropriate for them. For example, pupils are asked to practise throwing and catching in pairs and to choose from a range of different size balls and also to decide how far apart they are going to stand.
- Reciprocal style – pupils work in pairs, with one performing a skill against criteria provided by the teacher. The partner provides feedback using the criteria. The teacher communicates with the observer. For example, pupils take it in turns to swim one breast-stroke width of the pool. Their partners observe using criteria listed on a laminated work card and give feedback to help improve each other's stroke. The teacher discusses the quality of the stroke with the pupil who is observing.
- Guided discovery – the teacher sets tasks or asks questions that guide pupils towards the correct answer or successful performance of a skill. It encourages pupils to make their own decisions about,

for example, the best stance in order to hit a forehand, the most stable base for a headstand. See the example below from Gloria's class.

- Problem solving – this also encourages pupils to seek their own solutions but invites alternative solutions rather than a single right answer; for example, finding many different finishes to a forward roll, ending a dance routine with three points of contact with the floor, finding different routes to dribble through an arrangement of cones.

Reflective activity

- Which of the styles above would have the potential to promote interpersonal learning?
- How far would each of the styles above accommodate sequential and random processors of learning?

Gloria is teaching gymnastics to Year Four. The class is working on balancing using their head and hands. Most are attempting headstands. Gloria asks them to think about the position of their heads and hands and to try positioning them differently (in a line, in a triangle with head at the apex, in an inverted triangle with hands in front of the head) and they then discuss which is the most effective. She then asks them to try different leg positions – tucked up, straight, straddled and split – and to decide which are the easier ones.

The class watches several demonstrations of different headstands and discusses how to create a stable base using a triangle. They then consider the relative difficulty of different leg positions and how to make the performance of this skill look good.

- What style is Gloria using?
- What National Curriculum outcomes is she addressing through this approach?

Reflective activity

Winston is teaching games to Year Three. He asks the class to work in groups and to design a game that involves throwing and catching and scoring using some kind of target. They have to plan their game so that it is high-scoring. Several groups achieve this by playing 4 against 2 after failing to score with even sized teams. One group keeps teams of three but achieves high scores by using a very large target area (a long bench) that has to be touched with the ball to score. One group chooses to use a very large ball.

- What teaching style is Winston using?
- What are the potential learning outcomes for the pupils?

While the use of a range of teaching styles has the potential to bring about a range of learning outcomes and accommodate different learning preferences, there is some evidence to suggest that much physical education teaching remains didactic and teacher-directed (Mawer 1999; Penney and Evans 1999; Curtner-Smith et al. 2001). This is consistent with OfSTED's (2005, 2009a) evidence that less effective lessons are teacher-dominated and that pupils' ability to analyse their own performance remains limited. This is not to deny the value of direct teaching approaches or teacher-directed activities, especially when teaching a specific technique (Alexander and Penney 2005) or when safety issues are significant. However, the use of open-ended and problem-solving tasks has the potential to accommodate different kinds of learners, and also to enable pupils to improve their ability to meet curriculum aims that go beyond skill acquisition. Providing opportunities for pupils to discuss, work out their own solutions and analyse their own and others' work is also vital if physical education is to contribute to learning in other subjects and to other primary curriculum initiatives.

Example

Kevin's school is committed to embedding the rights, respect and responsibility agenda across the curriculum. Working with Year Four, he asks them to plan their own game in which teams have to pass the ball and then score. Groups have to work out their own rules and are then asked to come up with sanctions for those who break the rules. Kevin then leads a discussion on what makes a sanction appropriate, what kinds of sanctions might be seen as unkind, and which might be seen as humiliating or otherwise inappropriate.

(This example is based on work in Hampshire schools on rights, respect and responsibility, at www.3hants.gov.uk/education/hias/childrensrights.htm.)

Example

Judith is working with a Year Two class in a large infant school. The Year Two team decides to focus on developing the pupils' ability to work independently and on improving their decision-making and problem-solving skills. They use a range of new resources including pictorial task cards, some of which are used sequentially, for example for work on individual challenges in throwing and catching activities, some of which can be selected at random, for example a range of gymnastics tasks related to balance. They also use video to analyse their own and the pupils' performance and target the use of reciprocal and problem-solving teaching styles.

(This example and those following are on case studies of good practice in primary physical education at www.qcda.gov.uk.)

Example

Melanie wants to use dance to improve literacy and to enthuse her Year Three class about creative writing. During the Spring half term, the class has a 45-minute dance lesson followed by a one-hour literacy lesson using the same topic. The pupils talk about their dances and then write about them. The chosen topic is monsters, in which expressing feelings through dance is important. Over the half term the dance develops from individual ideas and explorations to group dance, to the final stage where the whole class performs the dance together. Pupils are asked to talk about how their bodies move, about how they feel, how they think others might feel, and, later, about how the dance is structured and about the way the different groups interact with each other.

Variety and choice in learning and teaching

There has been some debate about how much teachers should try to give pupils the opportunity to work using their preferred learning style or whether they should be encouraged to widen the learning styles used. The case studies included in this chapter demonstrate that learning styles are about maximizing the learning potential of physical education as much as they are about individual learning preferences. While the opportunity to use a preferred learning style may well have its place as a tool to motivate disaffected pupils, it seems clear that the real value of using a range of learning styles is the increase in breadth of potential learning outcomes. At the same time pupils will be developing their ability to work in ways that would not necessarily be their first choice.

If pupils are to use different styles and intelligences the teacher needs to use a range of teaching styles. For example, a command style will give no opportunity for the use of interpersonal intelligence and little for the use of linguistic, although it will use kinaesthetic intelligence, while the use of reciprocal teaching can involve all three. A problem-solving approach may have more appeal for the random and intuitive learner than guided discovery, which may be more motivating for the sequential learner who prefers the clear guidance and sequenced tasks.

Example

Two Year Six classes are working on running, jumping and rolling. Martin and Angela use a video clip showing different levels of performance and ask their classes to watch and tell them what is good and what each performer needs to do in order to improve. They then record each other's performance using digital cameras and assess the recordings against a checklist that tells them what to look for at the start, during and on completion of the movement being filmed. They then set targets for improvement. Prior to this Martin and Angela discuss with their classes what counts as constructive criticism and how to comment in a way that will secure improvement without upsetting people. This strategy was used throughout the year at times when the skills were relevant to the lesson. It led to a significant improvement in pupils' ability to give and receive constructive feedback so that they went beyond comments such as 'That wasn't very good' to remarks such as 'That was a better jump – next time can you try to keep your legs really straight when you are in the air?'

- What elements of National Curriculum physical education are being addressed here?
- What cross-curricular work is being promoted?
- What learning and teaching styles are involved?

(Drawing on a case study of high-quality primary physical education based on work at Abbey Park Middle School, from www.qcda.gov.uk/987. aspx.)

The activity that follows prompts the teacher to consider the range of learners that may be found in a primary class. If all pupils are to gain both enjoyment and achievement from physical education, then a balance is needed between work using teaching styles that accommodate learning preferences and those that challenge them to widen their learning repertoire. The first will provide enjoyment but both are needed to maximize achievement.

Reflective activity

Jason is a lively boy with high energy levels. He finds keeping still for any length of time difficult and also has problems when asked to listen for any length of time. He enjoys high levels of activity and is able to sustain these over a period of time. He also works more comfortably if he is left to work out his own solutions to problems that he encounters in improving his physical skills and does not always respond positively to advice or intervention.

Ravinder is a promising badminton player who is part of an elite junior squad outside school. She is a reserved girl who practises assiduously at any task set, but who prefers to work on her own and finds group work difficult and frustrating. She is used to very structured training that goes through a carefully ordered sequence of preparation, skill development and match practice as well as fitness work that is directed by her coach. This means that she finds the more creative approach to games activities, with expectations that pupils will create their own games, difficult and often frustrating.

Ben likes to work through tasks in an orderly and sequential way and to be given clear instructions about what to do and the order in which to attempt things. He dislikes being asked to work out solutions for himself and will ask for help frequently. He asks a lot of questions but is not good at watching others and learning from them. He enjoys working with task cards that provide him with information and a constant reminder of what his focus should be.

Anne enjoys lessons where she has the opportunity to design and plan work to be performed. Gymnastics and dance are the highlights of physical education for her. She enjoys using music and will volunteer to bring music suitable for both dance and gymnastic routines. She also thrives on tasks where she is able to plan movement patterns and leads the design of the floor patterns for a group dance performance.

- How might the teacher meet the varied needs and preferences of the pupils described?
- What kinds of learning activities would enable them to work within their individual comfort zones?
- What would be needed to widen their range of learning styles?

Summary

This chapter should have given readers an understanding and appreciation of learning and teaching styles, of what they mean in the physical education context and of what they might look like in a specific learning activity. It has shown the relationship between learning and teaching styles and how they relate to the kinds of learning outcomes that are expected of National Curriculum physical education. The chapter illustrated how a range of teaching styles can broaden the engagement of a variety of learners and widen the range of their achievements to encompass the development of skill, the selection and application of skills, tactics and compositional ideas. It has also demonstrated the analysis and evaluation of performance, knowledge and understanding, including that related to fitness and health, and the ability to work individually and in groups. To summarize:

- Different teaching styles will produce different learning outcomes. Some teaching styles will limit the learning opportunities – for example the use of a command style will not enable a class to learn to analyse or evaluate their performance.
- Schools tend to favour particular kinds of learner by their very nature; therefore, in order to include all pupils and give the best possible opportunity for all to succeed, conscious efforts need to be made to enable pupils to use different styles.
- At the same time, pupils need to learn to use different learning styles if they are to make the most of future learning opportunities.
- The National Curriculum physical education expectations can only be met fully if a range of learning and teaching styles are provided for pupils.
- If teachers are to use physical education as a vehicle for promoting learning in other subject areas, or in relation to other initiatives, for example creativity or rights, respect and responsibility, then they will need to use a range of teaching styles and engage pupils with different learning styles.

4   Inclusion matters

Introduction

The National Curriculum specifies that inclusion refers to 'boys and girls, pupils with special educational needs, pupils with disabilities, pupils from all cultural and social backgrounds, pupils of different ethnic groups including travellers, refugees and asylum seekers, and those from diverse linguistic backgrounds' (QCDA 1999).

The Qualifications and Curriculum Authority's (QCA) curriculum review suggests that there is further work to be done in physical education:

> Provision for specific groups of pupils including those with disabilities and those from different ethnic and religious backgrounds needs further investigation. Schools now need to focus on targeting and on more effective provision, particularly for pupils with physical disabilities and those from different religious and cultural backgrounds.
>
> (QCA 2005a: 13)

The clear message for teachers is that they need strategies to ensure that all pupils in their classes are included and are able to achieve and progress, and that none is excluded from the learning process. This chapter will focus on knowledge and understanding about including different groups. It will enable the teacher to make informed planning decisions on teaching and learning approaches that maximize inclusive and equitable classroom practice. The chapter will look at inclusion related to gender, race and special educational needs, but the strategies suggested are equally relevant to the inclusion of other potentially disadvantaged or under-represented groups. It will also show how a whole range of simple adaptations can lead to more inclusive practice that can benefit all pupils, and not solely groups or individuals with identified needs. It will emphasize that, although there will be individual pupils whose needs can only be met if highly specific needs are understood, much good practice can be developed once it is recognized that providing good teaching for all is often more important than looking to provide different kinds of teaching for specific individuals. Finally, it will demonstrate that needs may be subject-specific and will change over time.

Key issues

Inclusion is related to other concepts such as social justice, equality and equity. It is about striving for reduced inequality and about equal opportunities for all pupils. While many issues are generic, some are specific to physical education.

There is a tendency to assume that the child will have needs irrespective of the subject area and that a need is something fixed, permanent and the child's defining characteristic. The reality is that 'our understanding of who we are, our identity, is composed of a variety of "selves". In other words each of us does not have a single, unified identity but instead we each have a range of identities, we have multiple identities' (Browne 2004: 60). Browne illustrates this interaction when she points out that young children's experience of gender is influenced by many other factors including ethnicity, culture, race, social class, economic status and physical ability. She quotes a nursery head teacher commenting on the issue of making assumptions about achievement:

> It's a bit like saying 'All Bengali boys are failing to learn to read', which is nonsense. With some Bengali boys it might be much more to do with poverty than race, actually, that they are failing. But there are also white boys who are failing to learn to read and there are white boys who are flying just as there are Bengali boys.
>
> (Nursery head teacher, Browne 2004: 9)

The equivalent in physical education might be to say that Asian boys cannot play contact games but are good at racket sports, a common assumption in the literature of some years ago and one that has been rightly challenged more recently.

Gender

Gender issues in physical education often run counter to the prevailing debates, which tend to focus upon the underachievement of boys (OfSTED and EOC 1996; Epstein 1998). Connolly provides an example of how girls can become excluded from activity opportunities.

> It [football] was also a particularly gendered activity, being played exclusively by boys and girls not only prevented from playing but also sometimes fearful of going near ... not only were girls routinely excluded from football games but also South Asian boys who had generally been constructed through racist discourses as inferior and effeminate. Only one South Asian boy, Prajay, was occasionally allowed to play, mainly because he was in the same class as the boys who controlled the football games.
>
> (Connolly 2003: 119)

Although there is little evidence of negative attitudes amongst primary school girls, there is ample evidence of factors that affect the attitudes of adolescent girls from which the primary school teacher can learn. Much of this relates to contextual issues such as the kit that girls are asked to wear, changing facilities and processes, and participating in cold unpleasant conditions (Williams and Bedward 2000; Youth Sport Trust 2000). These are also issues for younger pupils, especially towards the end of primary school, where many girls are reaching puberty and are very conscious of their bodies and their appearance. These issues also arise because of the very early age at which children now engage with issues such as body image, weight and appearance. Inclusion in the physical education context is thus about much more than the learning and teaching process, important though this is.

It is important to remember that, at primary level, there are no significant physical differences between boys and girls, and girls tend to be developmentally ahead of boys. There are therefore no physical reasons for differences in performance between boys and girls although social mores and pressures still lead to differences in experience of physical activities and differing expectations of which boys and girls are aware from a young age.

Differential treatment of boys and girls from an early age in terms of approved play activities has been well documented. This tends to work to the disadvantage of girls in terms of their experience of games skills. Equally, boys are disadvantaged through perceptions of dance as an activity for girls, notwithstanding the impact of films such as *Billy Elliott*. Browne (2004) demonstrates that young children already have positioned themselves clearly as far as their own gender and gender-appropriate activity is concerned and that dominant styles of both masculinity and femininity are often reinforced by teachers. Gender is just as much an issue for the Early Years as for the primary school teacher.

That said, differences within each gender are likely to be at least as great as differences between genders and one of the most important messages for the teacher has to be to avoid assumptions about aptitude or interest based on gender, race or different educational needs, and to treat each child as an individual.

Cultural diversity

Cultural diversity issues in the context of physical education have focused on stereotyping, on cultural attitudes and practices that impact negatively on physical education experiences and on racism within sport. Stereotyping has included assumptions that Afro-Caribbean pupils will excel at physical education and sport rather than at academic subjects, that Asian pupils are physically frail and limited in their ability to engage in contact sports and that Muslim families are anti-physical education. The example given earlier (Connolly 2003) also illustrates how racial stereotyping can have a detrimental effect on inclusion. Two examples of how stereotyping and cultural assumptions can affect physical education are given here.

Cultural practices that have been high profile in the physical education context have often centred upon issues about the participation of Muslim girls. These have been about conflict between conventional physical education kit and expectations that girls should dress more modestly and about taking part in physical activity in the presence of unrelated males. Providing extracurricular opportunities that accommodate the need for Muslim boys to attend the Mosque after school and domestic expectations of girls has also challenged some schools. Just as with gender, avoiding assumptions based on ethnicity or religion is important. Miles et al. (2008) found that, among a group of Muslim families, attitudes to physical education varied significantly. Some were happy for primary-age daughters to participate in mixed-sex physical education without wearing the *hijab*; for others, this was acceptable provided that *hijab* and tracksuits were worn. Others preferred sex-segregated provision, especially for swimming. This highlights the need to involve parents and the community in formulating policy for the school or the individual class. It is equally important that the teacher appreciates that issues ascribed to Islam may actually relate to aspects of southern Asian culture rather than to the Muslim faith, which, contrary to popular belief, encourages both genders to be active physically.

Stereotyping in relation to African-Caribbean pupils derives from various myths that have persisted – such pupils find swimming difficult because they have heavy bones; they are good at dance because they have a natural sense of rhythm; differences in body composition mean that they are able to excel in athletics. Leading black sportsmen and women have been highly critical of the way in which they were encouraged to focus on sport at the expense of academic subjects and this has led to concerns that teachers are contributing to the poor attainment levels of some African-Caribbean pupils (Chappell 1995) through low academic expectations. These kinds of assumptions continue to influence school environments through the attitudes and beliefs of parents, governors, pupils and teachers. For the primary school teacher, balancing the positive opportunities that talent in physical activities may bring to some African-Caribbean pupils with the importance of encouraging high expectations and achievement across the curriculum is clearly important. Equally important is the recognition that while some African-Caribbean pupils may well fall into the gifted and talented category as far as physical education is concerned, others will share all the characteristics of others who find the subject difficult, including obesity, poor coordination skills and lack of confidence.

Special educational needs

Pupils with special needs represent an enormous diversity. For some, class-room needs do not apply in the physical education context; others who have particular needs in physical education have none in the classroom and a third group has very specific needs that extend right across the curriculum. While the term 'special educational needs' is generally used to refer to pupils who need additional support in order to achieve at school, gifted and talented pupils also have special needs and an inclusive curriculum should also meet the needs of these pupils. Research suggests that many teachers feel ill-prepared to meet the needs of pupils with special needs in the physical education context (Vickerman and Coates 2009). This may be a particular concern for the non-specialist primary school teacher. There are many resources currently available providing information about particular needs and practical strategies, teaching packs and lesson plans.

There will always be some individual pupils with complex and highly specific needs for whom specialist knowledge and understanding about their capabilities and the context in which they can be maximized will be needed. Meeting the needs of these pupils is beyond the scope of this book and teachers with such pupils in their classrooms should have access to help both within the school through the Special Educational Needs Coordinator (SENCO), from other agencies such as specialist support organizations and from specialized resources such as books and websites. For many pupils, however, inclusion can be achieved through relatively simple adaptations, many of which will benefit other pupils in the class.

Defining inclusion

Inclusion involves giving every child opportunities to achieve and succeed. Some writers have made a distinction between integration and inclusion. The former involves pupils fitting into the existing provision. In the physical education context this could often mean giving the child with special needs the task of keeping score or timekeeping or expecting all boys to play football and all girls to play netball irrespective of individual preference. It might also mean continuing to organize all extracurricular physical education after school rather than before school or at lunchtime and encouraging all to participate, even though this prevents pupils from some cultures from taking part because of domestic or religious commitments after school. Inclusion, in contrast, aims to enable all pupils to have access to opportunities to achieve. It does not necessarily mean treating all pupils the same.

Here are some examples. Consider how far they might be seen as inclusive practice:

Example

Daniel has very limited sight. A range of assistive technology enables him to take part in most curriculum subjects. He takes part in indoor physical education, although some gymnastics apparatus is off-limits for him, but during games lessons he stays indoors because staff are concerned that he may injure himself or another child.

Example

Asheefa wears *salwar kameez* and a *hijab* to school. Initially she was reluctant to take part in physical education because the school kit of shorts and t-shirt meant that she had to bare her legs in front of boys and male teachers. The head gives her parents permission to provide a tracksuit so that her arms and legs remain covered. Part-way through the year her teacher reports to the head that Asheefa is often absent from school on physical education days.

Example

Northend Primary has always run after-school football for boys. Some girls ask why they can't join in or have their own club. The head speaks to the teachers running the football club, who have no objection to girls attending although they have some doubts about their real level of interest. At assembly the head announces that football club will now be open to girls. There is some derisive laughter from a group of boys. No girls turn up the following week.

Example

Southwark Junior School offers a broad physical education curriculum for all pupils at Key Stage 2. Dance is taught for half a term in each year but there are constant complaints from teachers about the behaviour of boys in dance lessons. They are disruptive, lack motivation and make constant comments about dance being for girls.

It is clear that Daniel is not being given access to the same or an equivalent curriculum and, given the achievements of partially sighted people in a wide spectrum of physical activity and sport, that his disability is not, per se, a reason for excluding him from part of the curriculum. The remaining examples appear to offer the same curricular and extracurricular opportunities to all but the outcome does not seem to be one where all pupils are able to enjoy a comparable physical education experience. Together they raise a range of questions to which there are not necessarily any easy answers, but to which teachers committed to inclusive practice must give some thought.

Does access equal opportunity?

Asheefa and the example from Northend Primary provide clear evidence that the answer to this question is 'no'. Neither Asheefa nor the girls at Northend are denied access to the physical education curriculum or, in the case of Northend, to extracurricular football, but it is clear that access is not being given in a way that enables these pupils to benefit. In Asheefa's case, although she has full access to the curriculum, the conditions under which this has been provided, involving her dressing differently from the rest of the class, have left her uncomfortable and ill-at-ease to the point where she has effectively opted out of participation.

Southwark Junior School also demonstrates the potential gap between access and opportunity, illustrating how interactions between mixed-sex groups can challenge teachers to ensure that all have the opportunity to learn.

How far can school policy be inclusive so that individual pupils are not made to feel uncomfortably different?

Asheefa's experience is a good example of a situation that could be resolved easily to the potential benefit of other pupils. While shorts and a t-shirt are not unusual dress for physical education, there is ample evidence that pupils other than those from specific cultural groups find this dress problematic. Research has demonstrated on many occasions that physical education kit is a significant demotivator for girls (Williams and Bedward 2000; Youth Sport

Trust 2000). A change of policy to allow all pupils the option of kit such as long-sleeved tops or tracksuits would enable Asheefa to participate without feeling different and would also have a positive impact on other girls' physical educational experience. This would be a good example of working to the QCDA principle of overcoming potential barriers to learning.

How might working with partners and the involvement of visiting teachers address inclusion issues?

Southwark Junior illustrates an issue that faces many teachers. Non-specialist teachers may well feel that they lack the knowledge and experience to overcome the challenges presented here. Not only does the selection of suitable content present difficulties for the inexperienced, but changing the attitude of the boys is unlikely to be easy. One solution is to work with local partners and involve men from local dance organizations as in the example below:

Example

Cotner Farm Junior School was keen to engage the interest of Year Six boys in dance, at the time generally seen as for sissies or girls as far as the boys were concerned. They contacted AfroDance, a local company committed to work in education, who came into the school for two morning workshops. This provided the boys with male role models who were not only very good dancers but demonstrably extremely fit and, to the delight of all the pupils, thoroughly non-conformist in their attitudes to school and learning. DVDs of the company performing were presented to the school and these were used as stimuli for follow-up lessons. The status of dance within the school was transformed.

Working towards inclusion in physical education

Fundamentally, inclusion is about meeting individual needs that may arise as a consequence of particular personal circumstances such as gender, race or special needs or of a combination of circumstances.

For example, a strategy may offer girls an opportunity to take part in a single-sex after-school football club. It proves popular but three Muslim girls are unable to take part because they are expected to return home immediately at the end of the school day and two girls with special needs are not able to attend because they have after-school tutoring on the day of the club. The teacher organizing it assumes that they would not be interested anyway. If the club ran at lunchtime or before school, all would be able to take part.

Inclusion is about avoiding assumptions based on stereotypes or commonly held beliefs about particular groups. It is also about recognizing that all pupils have individual needs whether or not they are labelled as part of a specific group. Thus, as illustrated below, within one group of white boys with no known special educational needs, the range of interests and abilities in relation to physical activities will combine with differences in learning-style preferences, and with previous and current out-of-school experiences, to produce a wide range of learning needs.

Example

Darren swims for a local club and trains before school on three mornings a week as well as most weekends. James and Mark have both been taught to swim by attending holiday programmes at their local leisure centre. James loves swimming and would like to continue to swim outside school. Mark hates it and now that he has learnt to swim does not want to continue. Nathan cannot swim but loves being in the water and is overconfident. Jonnie is also a non-swimmer and dreads lessons as he is very frightened of being in the water. None of these boys would be seen as having any kind of special need or part of any targeted inclusion strategy, yet their individual needs in the context of swimming are very wide-ranging.

Jonnie, arguably, does have a learning difficulty in relation to swimming at least as great as that of other pupils in classroom subjects. His mother arranges for him to have intensive one-to-one tuition over the summer holiday and this transforms both his swimming capability and his confidence. The following year he swims happily with the middle ability group in his class, demonstrating that needs change over time.

A framework approach to planning

The STTEPS (space-task-time-equipment-people-success) approach is a common framework designed to help teachers to meet the needs of all pupils. Here a variation on that approach is provided as a tool to help the teacher to consider a whole range of strategies that could be incorporated into planning to make the curriculum more inclusive generally or for specific groups. A key feature of this approach is that the teacher adapts an aspect of the teaching-and-learning process or context in order to promote inclusion rather than trying to fit the child into existing practice. Each example enables the teacher to teach lessons that are differentiated in order to meet a whole range of different needs.

Space

- Change the size and shape of the working area. In some games situations, the smaller the playing area, the more challenging the task. Pupils who find controlling a ball through dribbling challenging need a large shared area or an individual space; those who have mastered the skill can be asked to control the ball in a group in a restricted area. In other situations, expanding the space adds to the challenge, for example throwing a ball over a longer distance.
- Adapt the scoring space. For example, when playing invasion games such as hockey or football, three different size goals can be placed along the scoring line. The children all have their own target goal related to their capability.
- Change the direction and pathways that pupils use. Pupils can be asked to create gymnastics sequences with a specific floor pattern. The complexity of the floor pattern can be used to vary the level of challenge from a short straight line that might involve just two or three actions, to a complex pattern that is both longer and demands many changes of direction.

Task

- Change the actions or tasks given and how the pupils are to do them. Differentiation by task is often used to meet different needs. Pupils can be set different tasks, selected to match individual or group needs, or they can be given a choice of task. The latter helps to promote individual responsibility in learning. The use of task cards in swimming or gymnastics enables the teacher to ensure that all pupils are challenged and given opportunities for success.
- Link changes to other dimensions such as timing and duration. The length of a gymnastics or dance sequence can affect the level of challenge. A talented Key Stage 2 child who is a competitive gymnast can be challenged to produce sequences of the length normally expected at Key Stage 4 GCSE level and to incorporate movement, stillness and changes of speed. A child in the same class with dyspraxia may be asked for a much shorter piece of work without change of speed.

Time

- Vary the time allowed for tasks remembering that longer does not always equate with easier. For example, a timed swim needs to be of short duration for the less able, while giving less time to pass the ball in a team game will make the task more difficult. The gymnastics example above also illustrates how a longer time duration is more challenging than a short sequence time.

Equipment

- Use different types of equipment and resources. The availability of balls of different sizes and materials can enable pupils with widely varying needs to succeed. A large sponge ball can be used for throwing and catching by pupils with a range of special needs and disabilities while smaller harder balls, such as tennis or cricket balls, present a much higher level of challenge within the same task and can provide the most talented with appropriate throwing and catching practice. Use of carefully chosen colours can assist pupils with visual impairments and also some pupils with dyslexia. Allowing pupils to choose their own equipment (with guidance if needed) will help them to become more aware of their own level of performance and of how to challenge themselves.
- Consider varying the play surfaces you use. If there is a choice between a hard surface and grass, the former may make activities accessible to pupils with physical disabilities and may make some activities easier for all pupils. On a hard surface all pupils will be able to take part in hockey or uni-hoc. The ball or puck will be easier to control for all. Pupils in wheelchairs can take part and any with mobility difficulties will be more successful than they would be on soft grass. Issues that can arise where girls dislike taking part in wet muddy conditions are resolved.
- Consider dress. This tends to be a gender or cultural matter. Many girls' attitudes to physical education are affected by requirements to wear physical education kit in which they feel embarrassed. Equally, families from some cultures will be unhappy with kit expectations that expose the female body. Tracksuits or other dress that can cover legs and arms can promote more inclusive physical education.
- Consider the appropriate use of ICT. The use of digital cameras to record work can provide visual feedback of benefit for all pupils but especially those who are visual learners, EAL pupils or those with language difficulties.

Groups

- Consider grouping people by ability. In order to maximize the benefits of using different equipment, some kind of ability grouping within the class may well be beneficial. Equally, ability groups facilitate varying tasks set. In other situations, however, there may be arguments for mixed-ability groups. For example, if the same task is set but different outcomes are expected, mixed-ability groups may well work. A reciprocal teaching approach may also work with mixed-ability pairs or trios, bearing in mind that partners with less physical competence may well be more than capable of analysing the work of their partners and improving it.

- Consider the appropriateness of mixed or single-sex groups. There is no simple single answer to the question of whether and to what extent single-sex teaching is desirable. There are undoubtedly situations where single-sex groups can help overcome some barriers to learning. That said, it has been argued (Browne 2004) that, in Early Years settings, there may well be a place for adults disrupting same-sex peer groups in order to move young pupils away from conventionally gender-typical behaviour. Teaching single-sex classes may well be difficult in many primary schools, although in larger ones it may be possible to combine classes from the same year so that pupils can be put into single-sex groups. Single-sex groupings within the class are an alternative that may address some gender issues although this will not resolve issues that may arise if parents want single-sex teaching for cultural or religious reasons.

Expectations
- Consider the range of outcomes that could come from a single task. A task such as 'find three balances using hands or hands and feet' could lead to outcomes that range from inverted hand balances from the very talented to supporting the weight on two hands and two feet with help from an assistant from a child with cerebral palsy.

Assessment
- Consider modifying assessment criteria.
- Use assessment for learning in conjunction with the above. Make good use of your assessment of pupils' current achievements to set realistic but challenging tasks. One of the key features of assessment for learning is that it promotes confidence that every pupil can improve.
- Do not underestimate pupils' ability to judge their progress provided that you give them clear expectations and criteria. Involvement of pupils in both peer and self-assessment is another important feature of assessment for learning that can be used very successfully in physical education. For example, use of pictures of balances together with indicators of good quality can enable pupils to assess the quality of each other's work and make suggestions for further improvement.

Support
- Consider how addressing different learning styles (see Chapter 3) might lead to higher levels of inclusion. The use of visual images can support learning – for example, pictures of different balances and linked balances placed around the room in a gymnastics lesson. These can assist with inclusion for pupils whose first language is not English, for pupils with hearing impairments, or for pupils with learning

difficulties whose language development may be behind that of their contemporaries and who may have difficulties in comprehending set tasks. Task cards with both words and pictures also promote learning for EAL pupils and for those who have difficulty hearing or with language.

- Consider initiatives such as peer mentoring or reciprocal teaching. Reciprocal teaching approaches involve pupils playing the role of teacher as well as performer. It can be an effective way of engaging all pupils in the learning process. Set up well, it gives all pupils ongoing access to support. For example, pupils may work in threes with two practising ball skills while the third observes. A task card has pictures of the skill performed correctly together with a list of points for the observer to look for.

Example

Year Five is playing an invasion game, working in ability groups that include:

- a group identified as gifted and talented, which plays for both the school and a local community team at football and netball;
- two groups that are achieving at the expected level for the latter part of Key Stage 2;
- one group that is just beginning to achieve the standard expected for Key Stage 2;
- one group that finds hand-eye coordination challenging.

The groups are organized as follows:

- One plays 4 v 4 in one-third of a netball court with a small hoop into which the ball must be bounced in order to score. They use a standard netball.
- Two groups also play using one-third of a netball court but score by bouncing the ball over the side line. They opt to play with a slightly lighter ball. One group plays 3 v 3 while the other, having tried that, opts to play 4 v 2.
- One group has a larger playing space and scores by throwing the ball to land beyond a line.
- One group uses a larger space and a large sponge ball and rolls the ball over a line to score.

This example demonstrates how variation in the size of playing area, equipment used and the use of ability groups can cater for a group that includes gifted and talented pupils, some with special educational needs and some that are performing at the level expected for their stage in schooling.

Example

Year Three is practising taking their weight on their hands. They are given a range of options on task cards and either sequentially work through them or choose one that is challenging but within their capability. Photographs from work done in the previous year are displayed on the walls. Options offered are:

- take weight on hands and feet with support;
- take weight on hands and feet;
- take weight on hands and one other body part;
- take weight on hands only;
- take weight on hands only with body inverted;
- begin on one body part, move onto hands and return to the same body part;
- begin on one body part, move onto hands and return to a different body part;
- repeat any of the above but using (a) a low padded table or (b) a narrow beam or upturned bench.

This example shows how the task can be varied to accommodate a very wide ability range and include pupils with major coordination and motor skill difficulties or physical disabilities. It also includes varying the equipment used to provide a further challenge.

Other approaches to promote inclusion

It has already been made clear (see Chapter 1) that physical education goes beyond what is offered within curriculum time. The importance of exercise, of making decisions about involvement in physical activities, of active and healthy lifestyles, permeates many aspects of school life, including informal playground activities, organized extracurricular sport and physical activity, classroom-based exercises such as those promoted by BrainGym and work with a range of partners such as PESSCL cluster schools, local sports clubs, coaches and development officers.

The playground has often been an area dominated by one group, generally football-playing boys, to the exclusion of other pupils. Girls, pupils with special needs and many boys are marginalized. A range of initiatives has been successful in giving all pupils access to active play. For example, Fair Furlong Primary School, as part of the PESSCL project, redesigned the playground in consultation with the pupils so that zoned areas included a fenced ball park for fast-flowing mini-sports, a more general activity area for basketball shooting, kingball, catch-up and 'piggy in the middle' and an area for quiet activities with seating and board games. Outcomes included a significant increase in pupils involved in a much wider range of activities that met a wider range of needs, with football no longer dominating the playground (PESSCL 2007a).

Provision for extracurricular physical activity and sport has often been limited by the availability of staff willing and able to run activities, especially in smaller schools. Increasingly partnerships of varying kinds enable schools to offer opportunities to a much wider range of pupils. Links with Sports Colleges give many schools chances to use the services of primary link teachers or specialist curriculum support teachers. Pupils identified as gifted and talented may gain from initiatives such as the Excellence in Cities programme or School Sport Partnerships. Within the school, the timing and organization of clubs can contribute to promoting inclusion by making activities available in ways that meet particular needs. This might mean offering single-sex clubs that meet the needs both of girls who are not confident performing in front of boys and also of girls from cultures for whom participating in mixed-sex activities can be problematic. Arranging for lunchtime activities can increase inclusion, not only by including those where cultural expectations make after-school involvement impossible, but also for other pupils who may have caring responsibilities in the home.

Summary

This chapter has discussed the difference between integration and inclusion, and the nature of inclusive practice. It has suggested a range of different ways in which teachers might adapt their approach.

To summarize:

- Inclusive practice involves learning activities that fit the child rather than expecting the child to fit in with what has traditionally been offered.
- All pupils have individual needs; therefore, the teacher who is committed to meeting the individual needs of the pupils in the class will be well placed to promote inclusive teaching and learning.

- Inclusion issues for physical education may be the same as those for other curriculum areas but there are significant areas of difference.
- Differences within groups tend to be as great as or greater than differences between groups so that popular assumptions about, for example, boys rather than girls, or Asian rather than African-Caribbean pupils, should be challenged.
- A small number of pupils will have complex and specialized needs that will only be met if the teacher can access specialist help.
- Many other pupils will have particular needs at some point in their primary school career, most of which can be met with adaptations to existing practice that are relatively easily made.

5 Assessing physical education in the primary school

Introduction

This chapter will look at assessment as a tool for learning. The different purposes that can be served by assessment will be discussed and related to different methods of assessment. There will be a particular focus on assessment for learning and on how assessment can help the pupil to progress. The principles of assessment for learning as set out by the Assessment Reform Group (2002), such as the promotion of shared learning goals and the development of the capacity for self-assessment, will be applied to specific examples from primary physical education. The relevance of assessment for learning to physical education requirements such as the evaluation and improvement of performance will be stressed and illustrated through examples. Reflective tasks will be used to focus the reader's attention on appropriate assessment strategies, on feedback to improve performance and on the relationship between strategy, feedback and assessment for learning. Examples will be provided of good assessment practice and how this has the capacity to promote further learning.

Purposes of assessment

There are currently no statutory requirements to assess in order to report achievement in primary physical education (DfEE/QCA 1999; Piotrowski and Capel 2000). However, primary schools do assess pupils' progress in physical education for a variety of purposes. Assessment supplies information that is used to help pupils to improve in all aspects of their performance by providing feedback to them and recording what they have achieved. A teacher can use assessment to help pupils to understand their strengths and weaknesses. It can also offer evidence of suitability for specific opportunities; these could include selection for teams and opportunities for school and club links. Assessment also provides feedback on the effectiveness of teaching programmes to help teachers to identify pupils' needs and aid their future planning.

Assessment opportunities give information to allow teachers to report to parents and other interested parties including governors, head teachers and other colleagues. These different purposes of assessment mean that it can be approached in different ways.

Approaches to assessment in physical education

Summative assessment is assessment *of* learning; it is a review of what a child has learnt over a unit of work, end of year or Key Stage and a judgement is made. Such a judgement is an evaluation in relation to set criteria, for example the learning outcomes of a unit of work or a 'best fit' National Curriculum attainment level based on achievement reached in several activities. Recording assessment of learning in physical education tends to tie in with the school's assessment policy and is often given a numerical value. However, there are several strategies to documenting assessment including pupil profiles, which can consist of commentaries, category tick boxes and comment banks. A teacher may comment on pupils' work at any point over the programme of study – this information can be used to build a profile of pupils' achievement to aid the writing of reports. For example, a child in Year Three may understand the importance of warming up in all activities, demonstrate and understand the vocabulary taught in gymnastics, excel in swimming by being able to swim two recognized strokes but experience difficulty in striking a ball in rounders. The recording of this information helps the teacher to keep track of the pupil's progress (in all aspects of performance including effort), which aids report writing, which might be carried out at the end of the year. Using tick boxes in profiles or reports requires a grading system to be matched against the learning outcomes of each module of work, or overall programme of study. Alternatively, comment banks consist of phrases and often include judgements on a progressive scale, such as these comments, which are based on acquiring and developing skills in gymnastics in Year Three:

- Able to practise a short sequence with quality of actions and transitions.
- Able to practise a short sequence of actions and transitions and now needs to refine movements.
- Is working towards practising a short sequence of actions and transitions.

In contrast to summative assessment is formative assessment, which is known as assessment *for* learning. Assessment for learning ought to occur all the time in the learning environment. It is rooted in self-referencing: a pupil needs to know where he or she is and understand not only where he or she wants to be but also how to 'fill the gap' in learning (Black and Wiliam 1998a). This involves both the teacher and the pupil in a process of continual reflection and review about progress. When teachers and peers provide quality feedback, pupils are empowered to take appropriate action. Teachers adjust their plans in response to formative assessment taking into consideration ipsative, norm and criterion referencing, which are also relevant to summative assessment.

- Ipsative referencing is linked to both summative and formative assessment in that it is centred on the child, measuring his or her progress. It indicates whether a pupil is improving or not, with the emphasis on comparing his or her previous performance with assessment irrespective of what others have achieved. The focus is on self-improvement and pupils can become motivated by seeing their own success (Carroll 1994; Williams 1996b). A teacher will often use ipsative assessment in reporting to parents in that they will describe the child's progress and achievement in comparison with previous attainment.
- The assessment approach of norm referencing is group-centred whereby an individual's performance is measured in relation to standards achieved by others. Pupils are therefore compared to each other, or to the objectives in a typical lesson, with some performing above and some below the average performance achieved. Assessment judgements may be made against the norms for particular ages so it indicates the relative position of pupils in a class or year group, with those being successful more likely to be motivated (Carroll 1994; Williams 1996b).
- Criterion referencing is centred on activity where performance is compared to a given expectation. For example, the National Curriculum assessment is criterion-referenced in that level descriptions (criteria) are given and a teacher makes a judgement about whether an individual pupil has met the criteria for a specific level (by giving a 'best fit' level at the end of Key Stage 2). Pupils need to understand what is required of them. It also enables comparisons to be made with others and a range of outcomes may be possible (Carroll 1994; Williams 1996b).

Assessment as a tool for learning

Given these different forms and purposes of assessment, in order to assess, teachers need to know what they want their pupils to learn and to recognize what is and what is not possible. Assessment should be on the basis of agreed, expected criteria (individually, group or activity based) which are known to pupils, and pupils should also know when they have achieved them. Assessment should therefore identify and build on every pupil's individual success, in addition to diagnosing their weaknesses and areas for future development. Teachers need to analyse such development and the progression involved in the learning process and provide opportunities for pupils to learn. An effective assessment process should be embedded in pedagogical processes rather than something that interferes with them. Evidence of attainment and achievement should then be recorded in a manageable reporting system.

Formative assessment has been given prominence in recent years particularly since the work of the Assessment Reform Group (2002: 2) who stated 'Assessment for learning is the process of seeking and interpreting evidence for use by the learners and their teachers to decide where the learners are in their learning, where they need to go and how best to get there.' The research conducted by the Assessment Reform Group led to the publication of ten principles to help guide classroom practice, these being that assessment for learning should:

- be part of effective planning of teaching and learning;
- focus on how pupils learn;
- be recognized as central to classroom practice;
- be regarded as a key professional skill for teachers;
- be sensitive and constructive because any assessment has an emotional impact;
- take account of the importance of learner motivation;
- promote commitment to learning goals and a shared understanding of the criteria by which they are assessed;
- ensure learners receive constructive guidance about how to improve;
- develop learners' capacity for self-assessment so that they can become reflective and self-managing;
- recognize the full range of achievements of all learners (Assessment Reform Group 2002: 2).

These principles were adopted by the National Strategy for Assessment for Learning whose aims were to support schools in developing their assessment processes as follows:

- Every child knows how they are doing, and understands what they need to do to improve and how to get there. They get the support they need to be motivated, independent learners on an ambitious trajectory of improvement.
- Every teacher is equipped to make well founded judgements about pupils' attainment, understands the concepts and principles of progression, and knows how to use their assessment judgements to

forward plan, particularly for pupils who are not fulfilling their potential.
- Every school has structured and systematic assessment systems in place for making regular, useful, manageable and accurate assessments of pupils, and for tracking their progress.
- Every parent and carer knows how their child is doing, what they need to do to improve, and how they can support the child and their teachers (DCSF 2008c).

With assessment for learning central to assessment in physical education it is worth investigating the strategies involved which aid the decisions about the next steps in learning and the ways in which pupils can be helped to make these next steps. Any action taken by the teacher to raise standards is enhanced when pupils are involved in decisions about their work rather than being passive recipients of teachers' judgements of it.

Using assessment to involve pupils in their own learning

When following a module of work, there is a need to identify learning objectives clearly based on an assessment and evaluation of the pupils' response to the previous lesson. These then need to be shared with them. This is because lessons remain better focused when teachers share the objectives with their pupils. Therefore, in order to fully involve pupils in their learning and to enable them to be involved in the assessment of their own learning, teachers should consider the following points, which will be explained in more detail in this chapter:

- Explain clearly the reasons for the lesson or activity, in terms of the learning objectives;
- Share the specific assessment criteria with pupils;
- Help pupils to understand what they have done well and what they need to develop;
- Show pupils how to use the assessment criteria to assess their own learning.

For pupils to be totally engaged in their own learning they need to identify any gaps between their actual and optimal performance. Pupils need to be able to work out why these gaps occur and they need to identify strategies that they might use to close the gaps. This is something that is best *done by* the pupils rather than *done for* them, or to them by the teacher, although the teacher's interchange is crucial to the pupil's understanding of what needs to be done next.

Assessment and sharing learning objectives

Planning and subsequently explaining and sharing the learning objectives at the start of each lesson is important to the success of the lesson in terms of a pupil's ability to make judgements about their learning. By stating what is to be learned, prefaced with the words 'What *I* am looking for . . .' (WILF), or alternatively, 'This is what *we* are looking for . . .', followed by the reason for the focus 'This is because . . .' (TIBS), the teacher will help to clarify the lesson aims from the outset, particularly if the language is understood by the pupils and is suitable to the unit or module of work being followed (Assessment Reform Group 2002; Spackman 2002). It is beneficial to separate the learning objectives from the task description to aid the organization of the lesson and keep the learning focus clear.

Indeed, keeping the description of the task separate from the learning objectives at the start of a lesson adds clarity, particularly as the description of the task may need careful explanation, which might take time. For example, it could include organizational aspects such as dealing with equipment or apparatus or involve different venues. Therefore, the objectives and task organization could be written and displayed on the wall to help students remember them, so if organizing the learning area does takes a long time, pupils can be reminded of what they are aiming to achieve. It is important that the learning objectives are revisited during the lesson. In the lesson plenary, revisiting them also helps to steer feedback. Long periods of pupil inactivity can be avoided if the teacher is creative in using the time available, for example informing the pupils about the task and its organization as they are getting ready for the lesson, or completing the plenary while pupils are changing.

Sharing criteria for success and modelling quality

Pupils need to understand what they are aiming for, so the success criteria should be shared. This could be qualitative, for example in gymnastics a teacher might say 'with pointed toes', 'stretch', 'hold your balance for at least three seconds', or measurable, for example in swimming 'swim a length of the pool', or a combination of both 'swim a length of the pool and kick from your hips'. The language used to describe the standard needs to be clear and reasonable. This could be relatively simple or more complex and accompanied by a demonstration, picture or film to model the quality or show 'the perfect model'. Involving pupils in their own learning helps them to recognize the standards they are aiming for, as well as informing them of the criteria for success. Pupils could also be responsible for the development of appropriate tasks, which helps them to progress to the next stage in their learning.

Reflective activity

By the end of a netball module in Year Five, most pupils are expected to be able to pass and shoot with control. They can identify and use tactics to help their team keep possession of the ball and take it towards the opposition's goal, as well as being able to mark their opponents and help each other in defence. Most pupils will understand the importance of warming up before playing netball and will be able to carry out warm-up exercises. They will also be able to identify aspects of performance in netball which require improvement and suggest and implement ideas to bring about such improvement. (DfEE/QCA 1999)

In considering the pupils' work in netball:

- What would you look for to ensure that pupils are working with control?
- Think about what other aspects you want the pupils to be able to do. What do these look like?
- How can you explain this to the pupils?
- How do you know if they have met the criteria?

A teacher needs to consider the tasks set for the lesson. Some tasks lend themselves well to developing reflection and pupil involvement in learning. Tasks that are markedly different from previous ones might encourage new reasoning more easily than tasks that are similar or repetitive. Tasks that require the learning of new skills, exploration, experiment or problem solving, such as the creation of sequences, dance motifs, adventurous problem-solving activities or game strategies, are suitable for probing questions such as 'What might have happened if . . .?' 'Why did you decide to do this instead of . . .?' 'What might you do next time?' Pupils can be helped to frame generic questions such as these to guide their thinking and task development. Further aspects of questioning are explained later in this chapter.

Reflective activity

Diane is teaching her Year One class, which is going to work on passing and throwing exercises in the playground. Before they go outside, Diane shares the learning objectives with the class. She writes key words and a 'good learners' list' (which shows the aims of what the pupils are able to do, what they will know and what they will understand) on the whiteboard. There are also pictures on the display board and she refers to them when she tells the class what she is looking for. The pupils complete the lesson and return to the classroom. Diane questions the pupils about the lesson and asks them if they think they have achieved anything on the 'good learners' list'. When she talks to them about their work, she asks them to think what would be 'even better if . . . ?'

- How should Diane use the assessment comments by the pupils to inform her planning for the follow-on lesson to address the next steps in their learning?

Self and peer assessment

When pupils have a clear idea of what they are aiming for, they can use their knowledge to guide their own assessment and to help others. In physical education, the goal is often classed as a 'performance' but this is not necessarily meant in a physical or practical sense, although it could be. For example, it could be the performance of a skill, an aesthetic performance, performance in a game or in terms of orally responding to a question. Being able to self-assess means that pupils will consider their performances against the success criteria and recognize what they need to do in order to improve. Sometimes, where movement is concerned, they may find this difficult because they may need to 'experience' what it 'feels' like to get it right.

Reflective activity

Julie is teaching swimming to her Year Six class. The group can all swim but are mixed-ability. The pupils are working on breaststroke and, in particular, breaststroke legs. The pupils know what they are aiming for because they have witnessed the perfect model, demonstrated by a member of the class. Several of the pupils are struggling with the stroke, swimming with pointed toes; the glide is restricted because they are not flexing their feet. Julie realizes that the pupils need to know what a successful leg kick 'feels' like.

- What can Julie do to help the pupils to feel what they need to do?
- How can the pupils assess their own performance?

Self-assessment works well with peer assessment, which can be very effective. Here, pupils will need help in identifying the criteria that make for a successful performance, or criteria that illustrate pupil understanding. Pupils will need training and guidance from the teacher to do this. For example, the teacher could steer the process by saying to the pupils 'Let's decide how anyone would know if this dance motif is good – what do you think they would see when looking at it?' When working reciprocally, it is important that pupils are given the opportunity to assess their peers and that teachers remember to give their feedback to the evaluator in order to improve his or her partner's work.

Establishing a trusting environment aids the process of peer assessment. This is essential to promote pupils' confidence, thinking and discussion skills. For peer assessment to work effectively, a teacher needs to consider how to balance the time required for pupils to be able to reflect upon their partner's performance, develop their skills of observation and analysis, be confident in seeking help if there is a need, and to try alternative ways of doing things without undue pressure. A teacher needs to adopt a supportive approach and allow pupils to experiment. For example, to encourage creative work, pupils will need to know that it is acceptable to look at a number of possible scenarios before opting for a particular course of action (see Chapter 7). Engaging in peer assessment can impact on a pupil's self-assessment as he or she has the opportunity to enhance his or her own understanding. A teacher may find it frustrating to 'stand back' to allow peer assessment, but it is vital to a child's development to do so. Here, a teacher needs to engage in a supportive role, which may involve prompts to steer learning.

Observation and analysis

In physical education, the use of cameras, camcorders and digitally recorded material can assist *all* in the assessment process (see Chapter 8). Indeed, the use of information and communication technology (ICT) can enhance self- and peer assessment and can aid the teacher by visually supporting feedback comments. Pupils can collaborate and make suggestions about each other's work. Pupils can also receive help in the evaluation of their own performance or that of others or a combination.

Reflective activity

Pupils in Alison's Year Two class are engaged in partner work. They are working on sequences involving rolling and jumping and are using apparatus that includes mats and benches. Alison gives the pupils time to practise their work. She then splits the class so that the pupils can watch their peers perform (half the class performing, while the other half watches). Alison gives the pupils criteria to look for as they observe. The pupils are given the opportunity to report their analysis and Alison gets the pupils to work on improving aspects of their partner work which she records by using a 'flip' camera.

- What aspects of feedback can Alison incorporate to help the pupils to observe and analyse the performance in order for the pair to improve?

Pupils will need to develop their evaluation skills, whether observing recorded work or a 'live' performance, as in the above example. The Early Years in particular will need guidance in how to observe and to show them what they are looking for.

Reflective activity

Think about the last time you engaged your class in evaluation activities which involved them watching others perform.

- How did you make sure all of the class engaged in the activity?
- What do you say to the pupils when you are asking them to observe and evaluate?

Some pupil performances for evaluation purposes may need consideration by the primary school teacher but this depends on the purpose of the evaluation. For example, evaluation in terms of formative assessment may require specific feedback to aid pupil improvement, whereas evaluation of a summative performance may draw on a range of points that have been addressed over a period of time. If pupils perform their work too early in the learning process, they may choose 'to play it safe', which may interfere with their creative learning process (see Chapter 7). It is essential to establish a supportive environment, as previously mentioned, so that pupils can feel that they can experiment in their work. A teacher might encourage the pupils by asking them to name three good things about their achievement in a lesson and what they would aim for in the future, known as 'three stars and a wish'.

Reflective activity

Ben is teaching a football lesson to a Year Five class. The class is working in small groups on drills. Ben wants each group to perform in turn, whereas the rest of the class have to evaluate. Some members of the class feel that they are not 'as good' as others and are reluctant to show their performances.

- How should Ben approach this situation?
- What are the possible outcomes?

Overall, evaluation exercises help the pupils to recognize the standards they are aiming for as well as assisting them in their ability to reflect on their progress. The development of reflective skills improves over time and advances for the pupils if they take an active role in the assessment process. It therefore helps if they have opportunities to self- and peer assess, to engage in questioning by listening to the responses of others and to learn to understand the importance of feedback.

Feedback

Feedback is the information a pupil receives about any aspect of his or her performance to aid improvement. Feedback by the teacher, self or peer helps pupils to realize where they are in their learning and gives them guidance as to what they have to do to reach the desired outcome, 'closing the gap' (Assessment Reform Group 2002). A teacher needs to allow time for dialogue with pupils as well as encouraging pupils to be reflective about their work, as previously mentioned. This dialogue needs to be sensitive to the pupils so that they feel safe and secure. Pupils benefit from receiving feedback either on a one-to-one or on a group basis. There are recognized characteristics of effective feedback that aid pupil learning. Feedback is effective when:

- it confirms that the pupils are on the right tracks and when it stimulates the correction of errors or improvement in performance;
- it focuses on the task and is given while still relevant and on a regular basis;
- suggestions for improvement give just enough help, which still allows pupils to use their knowledge – this is known as 'scaffolding' – they build on previous performance but do try to work and think things through for themselves;
- pupils are encouraged to find alternative solutions, rather than continuing in a manner that does not lead to improvement; and
- progress is made over a number of attempts (as opposed to feedback given on an isolated performance).

Over time, pupils can learn to see for themselves what they can do to improve their learning. Furthermore, feedback needs to leave the pupils thinking that they can achieve. The process of learning is as important as the product so in promoting learning the teacher needs to motivate and enable pupils to think and take risks in their learning. If comments are given too soon, the pupil could lose heart and play safe. Giving both precise and concise feedback and explaining why an answer or performance might be the correct one allows pupils to articulate their responses and improve their performance. Feedback needs to consolidate or reaffirm what has been learned and perhaps indicate alternative ways of trying something, which may involve prompting pupils to suggest ways in which they might make improvements. So suggestions for future work are sometimes referred to as 'feedforward'.

Reflective activity

In giving feedback in an Early Years dance lesson, Lesley said to one of the pupils, 'That part of your dance worked really well, I could see the difference between the shapes you made. Now can you show me how slowly you can move from one shape to another?'

*   What could Lesley specifically include in her feedback?

Inevitably, teachers need to allow time in their lessons to enable quality feedback to be provided. However, teachers should be mindful that too much time away from activity can also restrict the learning process. Balance between activity and feedback is therefore essential. Furthermore, pupils need the opportunity to address the feedback they receive, as well as the teacher checking that the pupil both understands and makes progress. If a teacher moves on to the next pupil too soon, there is no way of knowing how successful the feedback was. The teacher can engage the support of any other available adults to help in the feedback process, whether they are teaching assistants, coaches or volunteers. It is also helpful if pupils are given the opportunity to respond to their feedback, especially if a correction or further attempt has been suggested. To check that pupils have understood, teachers should engage them in questioning, which is an important strategy of both assessment *for* learning and assessment *of* learning.

Questioning

As well as finding out what pupils know and understand, asking pupils questions helps to develop their thinking skills. However, to ensure that questioning does promote thinking, there are some pitfalls to consider. For example, it is common practice for teachers to ask questions and immediately take the first response (Rowe 1974) or to answer the question for the pupil if the pupil does not give the 'required' answer (Black and Wiliam 1998b), or by moving from pupil to pupil in quick succession; these approaches inhibit pupils' thinking and are unproductive in the learning process. This is particularly the case if pupils do not respond with the required answers; if their offerings are instantly dismissed, opportunities to promote their learning are lost, as well as potentially leaving them with negative feelings, due to their thinking that their contributions are not valued. Thinking time should be incorporated and teachers can vary the questioning experience by operating a 'hands-up' or 'hands-down' approach (asking specific pupils what they think). For those pupils who do not want to respond, it could be a case of their not wanting to get the question 'wrong'. It may help to give them longer to think and return to them, or ask if they agree with another pupil's response and if so, why? This allows an opportunity for these pupils to build on a previous answer or to explain what they liked about another pupil's reply.

Reflective activity

Think about the last question and answer session you held in your physical education lesson.

- How much time did you allow before you accepted the first answer?
- How did you respond to the pupil who did not give the answer you were looking for?

Closed questions, which require factual, lower order answers, are a useful tool for checking knowledge. Open questions, which require lengthier responses, such as explanations, descriptions and comparisons, help the teacher to check pupils' understanding. In addition, open questions can promote physical literacy through the use of language. Through open questions, pupils can be encouraged to engage in higher order thinking which encourages pupils to consider alternative strategies. To promote thinking, pupils need to feel that they can respond, so it could be a case of a teacher telling the pupils that there will be no wrong answers.

The work by Bloom (1956) regarding the classification of thinking skills and the value of questioning, known as Bloom's taxonomy, is useful for the primary school teacher when planning key questions to promote learning. Pupils can be helped to develop deep thinking skills by exposing them to a variety of question types over their programmes of study. Table 5.1, based on Bloom's taxonomy, illustrates different levels of thinking (which progress from lower to higher order) and possible types of questions. These questions can be utilized in all aspects of assessment in physical education and include checking for pupil understanding, helping them to make connections and challenging their thinking.

Whilst teachers need to be mindful that they do need to build in time for thinking skills, as previously mentioned, there should be a balance between time for activity and time for reflection. It is important that some attention is given to developing listening skills. Pupils should be encouraged to talk to each

Table 5.1   Levels of thinking and possible types of questions

Lower Order	**Knowledge** Pupils are able to give factual answers and recall information	What is . . . ? When did . . . ? How did . . . happen? Why did . . . ? Where is. . ./was. . . ? Can you name . . . ?
	Comprehension Pupils are able to make sense of information	Can you explain in your own words . . . ? What do you think . . . means? Which movements show. . . ? Can you explain what is happening in this game . . . ? What can you say about . . . ? Which is the best answer. . . ?
Middle Order	**Application** Pupils are able to use information; for example, they know and understand the rules of a game and they can apply the rules in a practical setting	How would you use . . . ? What moves would you select to show. . . ? How would you show your understanding of . . . ? What approach would you use to . . . ? How would you apply what you have learned in this skill to . . . ? What other way could you plan to . . . ? What would result if . . . ? Can you make use of those players to . . . ?
Higher Order	**Analysis** Based on their knowledge and understanding, pupils can break information into parts, they can spot patterns – they can have alternative ways of viewing things, they are able to identify reasons and justify their answers	Can you identify the different shapes . . . ? What ideas justify . . . ? How would you categorize . . . ? Can you make a distinction between . . . ? What is the relationship between . . . ? What is the function of . . . ? What evidence can you find . . . ? What conclusions can you draw . . . ? What is the theme . . . ?
	Synthesis Pupils can draw information together, they can make connections, find alternative solutions and come up with new ideas	How would you improve . . . ? What changes would you make to . . . ? What would happen if . . . ? Can you extend that answer? Can you propose an alternative . . . ? How would you design . . . ?

(Continued overleaf)

Table 5.1 (continued)

	How could you maximize/minimize . . . ?
	What could be combined to improve/ change . . . ?
	Can you predict the outcome if . . . ?
Evaluation	
Pupils can identify and discriminate between various elements of practical performances or ideas; they can present their opinions and use evidence to support their decisions; they can make judgements about work and they can comment on quality	Do you agree with the actions . . . ?
	What is your opinion of . . .? (Explain your reasons)
	Can you give reasons for the importance of . . . ?
	Would it be better if . . . ?
	Why would you recommend . . . ?
	What choice would you have made?
	What would you select . . . ?
	How would you prioritize . . . ?
	How do you feel about . . . ?
	How would you justify . . . ?
	Why was it better that . . . ?

other about their progress, even if this happens as pupils change at the end of a lesson. Pupils could be encouraged to lead evaluative lesson plenaries, which also help to develop their leadership skills.

Reflective activity

Julie is working with her Year One class on short tennis. Julie demonstrates how to feed the ball to a partner who is to return. Julie observes the class. She notices that one girl is helping her partner and hears her asking 'What are you finding difficult?' 'What can I help you with?'

- What level of thinking is the child asking her partner questions demonstrating?
- How could Julie intervene to assist both pupils?

Summary

This chapter has focused on assessments that may be *of* learning (summative) or *for* learning (formative). A major focus has been assessment as a tool for learning that benefits from:

- the involvement of pupils in the process;
- sharing of learning objectives and success criteria;
- use of self- and peer assessment;
- the ability to observe and analyse;
- effective feedback (from the teacher or another pupil);
- use of relevant questions.

These elements of assessment are essential for pupil progress.

6 Moving to learn: cross-curricular opportunities

Introduction

This chapter will focus on physical education's potential contribution to cross-curricular or linked learning. Its context is a perception that physical education is hard to link with other subjects (Kellam and Whelwell 2009) although the reality is that physical education offers a multiplicity of opportunities for cross-curricular work. Independent subjects are a vital part of the curriculum but learning is strengthened through the contribution of cross-curricular studies (OfSTED 2006). Pupils are enlivened as they establish links between different subjects, which they do as they begin to comprehend new information and experiences (Alexander 2009; Rose 2009). It is these connections that assist pupils to develop their learning capacities and make sense of their environments (OfSTED 2006). The chapter will consider three approaches to cross-curricular work. First, topic-based teaching will be discussed; that is, the use of a theme as a focus for work in different subject areas including physical education. Topic-based approaches, where several subjects contribute to learning key concepts, have begun to reappear in primary schools following the publication of *Excellence and Enjoyment* (DfES 2003b) and have been recognized as aiding pupils' development and learning (Alexander 2009; Rose 2009). Secondly, the use of physical education to reinforce learning in other subjects will be considered. For example, data-handling skills from mathematics can be used in recording and analysis in athletics, while learning about map work in geography can be reinforced in orienteering activities within an 'outdoor and adventurous activity' (OAA) unit of work. Finally, the contribution of physical education to the teaching of essential cross-curricular skills such as critical thinking, personal and social skills, sustainability or health and wellbeing will be examined. Examples of good and innovative practice will be provided throughout, together with key questions to prompt reflection and analysis.

Curriculum design

Flexibility in curriculum design is key to successful cross-curricular work. Since the introduction of the National Curriculum in 1988 there has been an emphasis on teaching through individual subject disciplines whilst addressing government-driven initiatives. This has left little room for freedom in terms of school-based curriculum innovations. It is important to bear in mind that many schemes of work, which were written to support the curriculum, are not requirements but optional approaches (DfES 2003b). Recently, response to perceived curriculum overload and other pressures has led to statements from government departments (DfES 2003b) and others (Alexander 2009) reaffirming the autonomy that teachers have over what to teach and how to teach it.

The DfES (2003b) has encouraged schools to look afresh at what they offer to pupils and at how they organize learning, through scrutiny of their organization, of the timetable, the school day and week. Teachers have been prompted to consider how they could be innovative and enrich the learning experiences of their pupils. The message is clearly that, while teachers have to address relevant programmes of study, they have considerable freedom in doing this in ways that meet the particular needs of their pupils and that National Strategies may be used at a school's discretion.

Approaches to organizing the curriculum in terms of content and how and when it is taught are varied: there are no particular rules to adhere to (with the exception of the programme of study). For example, the timetable can be split into different periods of time, from 30-minute or hourly lessons to a half or full days, or even over a week.

Example

The normal timetable for Year Five is suspended so that they can take part in a 48-hour unit based on the theme of 'How we used to live'. This includes a sleepover in the school hall that enables the pupils to experience life during the Blitz in World War II. One afternoon is given to physical education in which pupils are given a range of carefully chosen equipment from the 1940s and 1950s and set a variety of games-making tasks. They create their own net/racket and invasion games.

Classes might experience different teachers. It is 'normal' for the primary school teacher to be responsible for a single class but there are many opportunities to bring in outside expertise or for internal class exchanges to expose pupils to as wide a range of expertise as possible. Curriculum content can be taught in a number of ways, which include specific subjects, clusters of subjects or topic work across the whole curriculum. Overall, the extent to which cross-curricular teaching is embedded in the primary school curriculum has the potential to be wide-ranging.

Cross-curricular themes and physical education

Schools that have embraced cross-curricular opportunities to high acclaim have done so by presenting a mix of individual subject teaching and topic-based work (DfES 2003b). Topic-based work is that which can be taught in different contexts across the curriculum and is also known as theme- or project-based work. To fully engage with cross-curricular work a teacher needs to think beyond separate subject boundaries and consider the learning as a whole. Here a variety of skills, knowledge and understanding can be developed through different themes. Physical education can contribute a host of opportunities for learning in this way. The starting point may be a physical education lesson that becomes the catalyst for learning in other subjects.

Reflective activity

Lisa is teaching her Year Six class a traditional Greek dance, which is to be the catalyst to make connections to other subjects. The pupils learn about the location and terrain of the country through geographical links and they learn about traditional Greek costume through art. In history, the pupils learn about the start of the Olympic Games, which is then covered in physical education through athletics. The pupils learn about the different events that make up the Olympic Games. Lisa selects three events, which consist of a run, a throw and a jump. The pupils split into teams; each team is given a name of a country and pupils cover the events over subsequent lessons.

- Are there any other subjects which could be linked here?
- If so, what activities could pupils do to enhance their learning?

Alternatively the starting point may be a theme to which different subjects are then linked – for example, 'Down Your Street' as shown in Figure 6.1, where each subject makes its own distinctive contribution to the chosen theme. In this case, traditional playground and skipping games, drawing on local traditions, constitute the physical education component.

Figure 6.2 provides a further example of a theme – in this case 'toys' – used to draw together work across a number of different subjects. In this example,

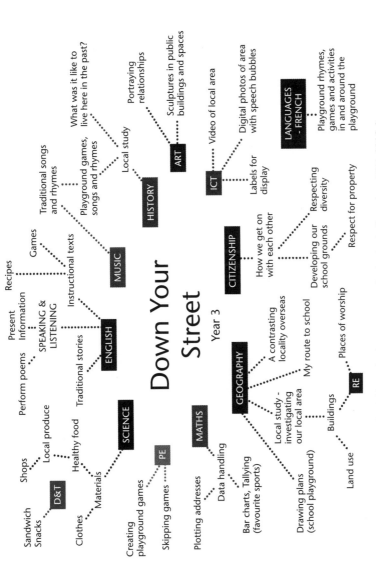

Figure 6.1 A blueprint for a cross-curricular topic (based on TDA 2010a).

Down Your Street

Year 3

ENGLISH
- Present Information
- Recipes
- Games
- Instructional texts
- SPEAKING & LISTENING
- Traditional stories
- Perform poems

SCIENCE
- Shops
- Local produce
- Healthy food
- Clothes
- Materials

D&T
- Sandwich Snacks

MATHS
- Data handling
- Plotting addresses
- Bar charts, Tallying (favourite sports)
- Drawing plans (school playground)

PE
- Creating playground games
- Skipping games

GEOGRAPHY
- A contrasting locality overseas
- My route to school
- Local study - investigating our local area

RE
- Places of worship
- Buildings
- Land use

CITIZENSHIP
- How we get on with each other
- Developing our school grounds
- Respecting diversity
- Respect for property

MUSIC
- Traditional songs and rhymes
- Playground games, songs and rhymes

HISTORY
- What was it like to live here in the past?
- Local study

ART
- Portraying relationships
- Sculptures in public buildings and spaces

ICT
- Video of local area
- Digital photos of area with speech bubbles
- Labels for display

LANGUAGES - FRENCH
- Playground rhymes, games and activities in and around the playground

English	Mathematics	History
Pupils will write a simple account about the trip to the Toy Museum that had a range of toys and puppets on display from a range of historical periods. They will think about what they did when they were there. They will write about what they learned and what their favourite toy was. Some pupils will go on to write about the different materials used to make the toys.	Pupils will sort toys according to their size. They will create graphs or charts that record the numbers of toys of different dimensions.	Pupils will look carefully at pictures of pictures/photos of pupils in the past playing with toys and discuss on the carpet what they can see – and what clues they provide about life in the past. The pupils will write a small paragraph about the pictures they see.
Science		**Design and technology**
The pupils will look at a range of toys and discuss what material they are made from. Why? How do they feel? Smell? Look? They will then draw and label these toys in their books. The labelled drawings will be used as part of a writing task (see above).	**TOYS** (Year Two)	The pupils will work individually to design a glove puppet. They will think about who they are making it for and what design it will have to be.
RE		**PE**
Pupils will use a selection of dolls to begin a discussion about different cultures and some of the festivals associated with them.		Pupils will use their glove puppets as a stimulus for dance based on puppet movements and puppet 'conversations'.

Figure 6.2 Toys as a cross-curricular topic for Year Two.

work in one subject leads on to work in another. For example, glove puppets made as part of work in design and technology become the stimulus for work in physical education, in this case in dance. Work in history and science provides the focus for writing, extending the reports that pupils have already written about their museum visit.

Using physical education to reinforce learning in other subjects

An important aspect of cross-curricular work involves using one subject to reinforce learning in another. Physical education offers many opportunities for this kind of work and provides the teacher with the potential to overcome some of the challenges of an overcrowded curriculum. For example, a physical education lesson with young children can contribute as much to their language as to their physical development and learning. An apparatus lesson in gymnastics can provide opportunities to explore and refine skills such as climbing, swinging, jumping and rolling. At the same time the teacher can develop and reinforce understanding of key language concepts such as over, under, round, through, above and beneath. Similarly, mathematical concepts, such as rotational and reflective symmetry, can be taught or reinforced in a gymnastics lesson through, for example, discussing whether balances or rolls are symmetrical and, if so, the kind of symmetry involved.

Reflective activity

Sunita is teaching mathematics to her Year Three class. They are covering numbers and measurements and are starting to learn how to present numbers in different formats. Sunita decides to link this work in mathematics to physical education. She does so by linking with athletics where pupils are measuring how far they can throw bean bags. They subsequently record this data. They cover different ways of throwing, including underarm, overarm and from the chest. They work on throwing from standing positions and with run ups. They learn how to measure, from the point of release to where the bean bag lands, and record their results by adding them to a printed form. The pupils then work with this information and detail the information by producing graphs and then they compare their results.

- In what other ways can athletics be linked to mathematics?
- Can learning in athletics be linked to any other subject(s)?

Reflective activity

In art, Robert is working with his Year Five class. He is working with the pupils on developing their powers of observation. He asks the class to imagine a cartoon character. Pupils devise a comic strip, based on one character. Robert then encourages the pupils to think how they can bring the comic strip to life. He uses the work in art as a foundation on which to base a dance motif.

Robert differentiates the dance activities. Some pupils have produced comic strips which give a clear story from which the pupils can be creative and develop their own dances. Others have found the task a challenge, so

Robert provides a copy of a comic strip and guides these pupils through a dance, building the motif frame by frame.

- What are the possible learning outcomes of this approach?
- How can links between art and dance be developed?

Both of the above use physical education to reinforce learning specific elements of a different subject. There is a slightly different, more integrated approach to teaching one subject using another in which the starting point is how one subject can combine with another. For example, a unit of work could be planned that brings geography together with OAA, or, as the example below demonstrates, teaching modern languages within a physical education lesson.

Example

Mark organizes Year Two into groups, each of which wears bands of a different colour. He uses the 'traffic lights' game to introduce colours in French and follows this with activities in which the group colour, in French, is used to identify the order of starting and stopping. He also uses the '5, 4, 3, 2, 1' approach to gain the pupils' attention to teach numbers in French. Praise and simple commands are also given in French.

A further example shows how swimming can be linked with science:

Reflective activity

Parimal's Year Six class is learning about water safety and about the workings of the body. He is teaching the pupils how to retrieve objects from the bottom of the pool. He talks to the class about holding their breath when they are under the water. Some pupils struggle with their breathing, not only in the water safety activities but also when swimming on the surface. Parimal talks to the pupils about the respiratory system and follows this up with a classroom experiment to establish for how long each individual can hold their breath. This leads to further discussion about the causes for these differences.

- How can these links between swimming and science be developed?
- Can these aspects of science be connected to any other activity?

Key cross-curricular themes and skills and physical education

Key themes and skills have been a part of each version of the National Curriculum and have also featured in various National Strategies. Themes include health, wellbeing and sustainability and skills include thinking skills, problem solving, personal and social skills.

Cross-curricular themes

One theme with a very obvious link to physical education is health and wellbeing, a key part of the *Every Child Matters* agenda. Pupils' health remains at the forefront of educational debate – indeed 'being healthy: enjoying good physical and mental health and living a healthy lifestyle' are among the outcomes of the *Every Child Matters* (DfES 2003a: 6) agenda. As Alexander (2009) points out, if pupils are unhealthy they are less likely to do well in school. For example, their ability to concentrate will diminish – learning across all subject areas will suffer as a consequence. There has been much concern over recent years about the issue of the rise in childhood obesity, resulting in the call for more time and resources to facilitate and promote exercise and activity in schools (Harris and Cale 1997). Physical education can contribute to pupils' understanding of the benefits of leading a healthy and active lifestyle through the way that it is taught, through extra-curricular activity opportunities and through cross-curricular links. They can learn about the importance of a healthy diet and the dangers of eating disorders leading to anorexia or bulimia nervosa, the functioning of the human body systems as well as the ways in which diseases are caused (DfEE/QCA 1999; Rose 2009).

Reflective activity

Year Two pupils are working on exercise and health in their science lessons with Julie their class teacher. Julie wants the pupils to link scientific theory to their knowledge and understanding of fitness and health in their physical education lessons. Julie explains that a heart is a ball of muscle which is working all the time. She asks the pupils to find their pulse and then questions them as to how they can make it go faster or slower. Julie sets the pupils a running task and jumping task. She asks the pupils to feel their pulse again and questions them about changes they have noticed.

- How might the pupils recognize and describe how their bodies feel during exercise?
- What other activities could the pupils do to realize that their pulse changes?

Reflective activity

Julie progresses her Year Two class to thinking about how bodies move. She asks the class to look at a skeleton. She then asks everyone to bend their arms and feel their biceps. Julie uses the skeleton to illustrate what she has asked the pupils to do. She explains to the pupils that the skeleton is a frame for muscles and other body parts. Using puppets as well as the skeleton as examples, she explains the similarities of the two in terms of the way they are built but explains that the puppet is unable to move without strings. Julie explains that muscles are what allow us to move and that we all have them, even the weakest of us. She asks the pupils to take a closer look and feel at what happens when they bend their arms.

- What physical activities could the pupils do to further their understanding?
- How does this lesson address issues of health education?

Developing pupils' understanding of their physical development and health through being active contributes to their wellbeing. Generally, wellbeing relates to the positive mental and physical state of a child and it is 'underpinned by the acquisition of a range of personal skills and dispositions that support [a child's] learning and development' (Rose 2009: 12). The connections between health and wellbeing are immense, so attending to children's wellbeing means addressing their health, physical and emotional welfare (see Chapter 2), as well as maximizing their learning potential through effective teaching, which addresses individual needs (Alexander 2009).

Another current key theme is that of sustainability. Taking a whole-school approach requires input from all subject areas. Teachers have to monitor and manage learning effectively across the curriculum. Such an approach is taken to help pupils understand ideas and issues surrounding important matters such as sustainable development. There are many factors to consider when teaching for sustainable development due largely to its different definitions. For the purposes of addressing cross-curricular learning in this context, sustainable development is about education for sustainability, or sustainable living. Sustainability could be used as the key concept drawing subject-based work together in the same way as shown in Figures 6.1 and 6.2.

Sustainable development can also be integrated into many aspects of the curriculum, particularly personal and social, environmental and health education (Robinson and Shallcross 1998).

Many primary schools are involved in sustainable development to some extent by operating 'eco' or 'healthy' schools thus linking sustainability with health and wellbeing. Here schools take on board a diverse range of issues. For example, they consider their environment, recycle and have their own vegetable gardens, promote health and wellbeing, as well as learning about the economy and operating enterprise schemes.

Physical education has an important contribution to make to cross-curricular work based on sustainable development. The most obvious links include any physical learning that takes place outside the classroom (see Chapter 9), whether in the school grounds or at an outdoor education centre, many of which are 'eco centres'. For example, when working in the natural environment, as part of OAA, pupils need to consider issues such as looking after natural habitats and learning how to keep safe. Both these issues link with geography from learning about maps and landscapes and how weather changes in different environments (DfEE/QCA 1999). Themes can be developed through a number of OAA, from orienteering to rock climbing, which include looking after landscapes and knowing and understanding the dangers of pollution.

Reflective activity

Year Six is studying the environment in geography and why places are like they are, for example studying locations such as exposed hillsides or sheltered coves. Mark links geographical fieldwork to physical education through OAA. The pupils go on a residential experience and attend an outdoor education centre.

Pupils learn both in the classroom and in the outdoors. They are learning about different types of rocks (their texture, permeability and appearance) and how they were formed. The pupils participate in rock climbing and Mark helps them relate the geographical class work to learning out of doors, as the pupils see, feel and work with the rock.

The pupils learn about the changing environment and the arguments for and against natural energy. Mark also links this to science, regarding the protection of living things. In particular, the pupils learn about wind turbines. To help pupils understand wind power, they do some sailing activities and they feel the strength of the wind against their sails in their dinghies.

- What questions should Mark ask to maximize the connections between the subject areas?
- In what other ways can OAA promote learning about sustainable development?

In addressing learning opportunities to help pupils appreciate sustainable development issues, there is a need to encourage pupils to think beyond their immediate vicinity and familiar environments. Pupils can be encouraged to think about global issues through theme-based units of work that include dance, as in the example below.

Reflective activity

All years are engaged in a wildlife awareness project and Grace is using the rainforest as a topic for her Year Four class. Grace makes connections across the curriculum. Pupils work on sound and rhythm in music and compose short tunes. In English, the pupils consider vocabulary which could describe life in a rainforest. They then use this information to write poems. The poems are then presented as the main stimulus for small group dances. Pupils think about key words or images from the poems as their starting point.

Lee has decided to focus on endangered species with his Year Five class. He wants the pupils to develop their critical awareness and thinking skills. He opens the dialogue with questions such as 'What would happen if . . .?' The questioning leads to the pupils writing stories, and, in art, pupils design and make animal masks. Based on their stories and masks, Lee helps the pupils to choreograph a dance. The pupils think about the movement their selected animal makes. Lee encourages the pupils to think in terms of quality, so the movements become more than 'mimicking' animal movements.

- What learning outcomes can be expected from these two approaches?

Cross-curricular skills

Cross-curricular learning can contribute to the development of essential skills such as thinking, problem solving, and personal and social skills. Using thinking skills across a curriculum can help pupils to develop their knowledge and understanding in a deeper and more meaningful way. Cross-curricular opportunities can complement what is taught in individual subjects and contribute to pupils' learning skills as pupils adapt their learning in new situations.

In establishing environments for learning, it helps if exciting opportunities are offered, which engage pupils and develop their enquiring minds. Physical education contributions to cross-curricular learning can be enjoyable and challenging and geared towards stimulating critical thinking.

Example

Year One is working on the theme 'creatures of the sea'. Leanne, the class teacher, is incorporating a variety of subject disciplines into the topic and she is assisting the pupils to develop modes of enquiry. She links learning to geography and guides pupils to see how much of the Earth is covered by water as they look at globes and maps. She asks the pupils 'What do you think it is like to live in the sea?' As the topic develops, the pupils make further links to art where they do drawings, sculptures and collages of creatures and to music where pupils experiment with different instruments to find sounds which suit a chosen creature. Against a backdrop of the artwork and to the recordings of the pupils' music, the pupils develop a dance. Leanne encourages the pupils to think about how their creature would move and uses vocabulary to help them think, such as darting, drifting, rising, falling, weaving and hiding. They use whole and isolated body movements and gestures to show how they are thinking and feeling.

- What questions does Leanne need to ask the pupils to promote critical thinking?

Reflective activity

In dance, Year Two is being encouraged to move imaginatively and to think about the rhythm, speed and level of their motifs. Their stimulus for the dance has come from toys. With Mandy, the class teacher, the pupils have been investigating contrasting movements. In particular, the pupils have compared and contrasted the movements of a rag doll and a robot. Through science they have looked at forces and levers. In design and technology they have experimented with mechanisms and have selected various pieces of equipment to make their own robots. Mandy encourages the pupils to consider all of their learning; the pupils develop their ideas and work in small groups as they experiment with movement to create small group dances.

- What other resources could Mandy incorporate to enhance thinking?

Problem solving can readily be placed at the heart of much learning in physical education, through the judicious choice of teaching styles (see Chapter 3). Problem solving is a common approach in OAA where pupils may be asked to work in teams to find a way to negotiate an imaginary or real obstacle using equipment provided. Problem solving is also central to much gymnastics teaching when pupils are asked to find different ways of finishing a forward roll, balancing on a specified number of body parts or travelling along or around a piece of apparatus.

Personal and social skills are key life skills that can be enhanced significantly through work in physical education. At the most basic level, social skills are developed through the need to share a working space in which the whole class is moving around.

Example

Jenny's Year One class is poor at using space effectively and the pupils often argue about who they are going to work with. As a starter activity she asks them to move about the space, first at a walk and then speeding up. She stops them each time they become clustered in one area of the hall and reminds them about looking for spaces to move into. She times the length of time they are able to keep moving without being stopped and each week the class tries to beat the previous week's record.

The second activity involves moving around and when Jenny calls out a number, the pupils have to get into groups of that size and sit in a space. Points are given to those quickest at sitting down with a bonus point to groups that see a child with nowhere to go and invite them to join their group.

The use of reciprocal teaching (see Chapter 3) also develops social skills through the need for cooperative behaviour and good communication.

Example

James gives his Year Four class task cards with pictures of different gymnastics balances. The pupils work in pairs. They attempt to copy as many of the balances as possible while their partners help them to improve the quality of each balance by giving them feedback based on the tips on the task card.

Personal and social education are often said to be at the heart of outdoor education (see Chapter 9), but the contribution of all physical activity areas should not be underestimated.

Summary

Approaching cross-curricular learning in the way illustrated by the case studies in this chapter (and the cross-curricular case studies in other chapters) helps to encourage teachers and pupils to engage in creative learning and to think 'outside subject boxes' (Rose 2009). OfSTED inspections focus on the extent to which a school caters for the needs of its pupils through a broad and balanced curriculum. Furthermore, schools are encouraged to offer a flexible and innovative curriculum that has links across the subject areas and adds value to the learning process (DfES 2003b). Previous OfSTED inspections led to the report *The Curriculum in Successful Primary Schools*, which detailed that 'good' cross-curricular links:

- strengthened the relevance and coherence of the curriculum for pupils;
- ensured that pupils applied the knowledge and skills learned in one subject to others, thus reinforcing their learning and increasing their understanding and confidence;
- made good use of longer blocks of time, enabling pupils to undertake sustained work on themes covering two or three subjects (OfSTED 2002).

Establishing and understanding the relationships between subjects contributes to pupils being able to learn more effectively, as there is an opportunity to embed skills and knowledge in significant ways to promote learning. Indeed, as pupils make connections between their subjects, they have the potential to recognize how they are making progress. Teachers can also assist pupils in helping them realize that some of their skills are transferable from subject to subject, as well as across a subject which gives them a different context for learning. This chapter has illustrated three aspects of cross-curricular work: theme/topic-based units that involve learning in a number of subject areas, reinforcement of learning in one subject within another and adding further dimensions to subject work through a focus on key skills.

7   Creativity in physical education

Introduction

Creativity has long been present in education in one form or another and often without conscious attention. The current emphasis on creativity began with the publication of the report *All Our Futures* in 1999 from the National Advisory Committee on Creative and Cultural Education (NACCCE) (1999), whose aim was to audit provision on the creative and cultural development of young people with recommendations for future practice. Initially building on the White Paper *Excellence in Schools* (DfEE 1997) which laid out objectives to improve education with a focus on recognizing the varied talents of pupils and seeing the potential in every child, *All Our Futures* laid a foundation for creative potential to be embedded throughout a school's curriculum. The report was taken up by the QCA in 2005 when *Creative Partnerships* (QCA 2005b; Sefton-Green 2008) continued to explore the relationship between creativity, culture and education, with particular exploration of creative learning. The agenda to keep creativity at the forefront in international educational settings is strong (Craft 2006).

In its simplest form, creativity involves the use of imagination and original ideas to create an outcome, although theorists argue that there are deep complexities surrounding its meaning and what it means to be creative (Fisher 2009). This chapter will clarify the nature of creativity, creative learning and creative teaching before focusing more closely on how the teacher can use physical education to promote creativity. The emphasis will be on teaching for creativity and on developing the creative capabilities of pupils, in line with OfSTED's (2010) finding that the best schools develop creativity in all pupils, irrespective of their ability. The potential of physical education to promote creative environments that encourage outdoor play, exercise, experimentation and managed risk taking, particularly in Early Years education, will be explored and illustrated with examples of good practice. Key approaches to developing creativity will be discussed with specific reference to their use within the physical education context. Examples of innovative teaching and learning together with reflective questions and prompts will be used to encourage further critique and development of practice.

The nature of creativity

Creativity in education can be perceived in different ways. Common misconceptions include that it is confined to the arts, that only some are capable of being creative or that creative teaching means a lack of discipline (NACCCE 1999; Cropley 2001). Due to the different contexts and theories of creativity it can be difficult to arrive at an agreed definition.

Some describe the definition of creativity as elusive (Cropley 2001; Fisher 2009; OfSTED 2010). Indeed, the NACCCE (1999: 28) described the difficulty in providing a definition for a process covering a variety of personal styles and a wide range of activities. Drawing on their understanding of creative processes and creative language in educational contexts, their definition reads 'Imaginative activity fashioned so as to produce outcomes that are both original and of value'. The rationale behind this definition draws on characteristics of creative processes. For example, they describe imaginative activity as the process of generating something original through thinking or behaving differently to what was expected or from the norm, although directed towards some kind of purpose. Imaginative activity often involves play whereby pupils are given opportunities and encouragement to view situations from different angles to see if they can come up with alternatives. Pupils are encouraged to generate ideas, make connections and gain insight, perhaps in unexpected ways.

Example

A teacher who takes a creative approach to learning may start off teaching a particular theme. The topic is carefully planned and guided by the teacher as it is introduced. The teacher encourages pupils to question from the outset and to use their imagination to see what possibilities are open to them. The direction of both teaching and learning can progress and develop in many different and often unexpected ways. The pupils are encouraged to follow their thoughts, not necessarily working in linear fashion. The pupils are given opportunities to critically reflect on their ideas and consequential and subsequent actions.

Reflective activity

Ann starts a topic working on insects and mini beasts with Year One. The pupils imagine that they are sitting on a magic carpet and flying to a far-off land. Once they reach their destination they describe what insects they meet. Previous work had covered bees and caterpillars and Ann had incorporated stories and paintings; on this occasion she guides the pupils towards the discussion of butterflies. Through this discussion Ann encourages the pupils to use their imagination with prompts such as 'what would be even better if?' and this leads to a dance where the pupils work in pairs and cover the themes of matching, spatial awareness, changes of direction and speed. The pupils' work is video recorded and they are encouraged to evaluate their own work.

- If you were teaching this lesson, how would you do it differently?

All pupils are capable of being creative or learning creatively in physical education. The uniqueness of each individual brings the potential to produce something original. It is argued that there are different categories of originality (Boden 1990; NACCCE 1999) plus varying degrees of originality within them. The categories include:

- an individual category where work produced is original in comparison with any previous work by the same individual;
- a relative category where work is original in relation to a pupil's peer group;
- an historic category, which indicates work produced is unique in comparison to any others (NACCCE 1999).

In the primary school setting, originality is most evident in individual and relative categories.

Reflective activity

In an Early Years lesson, Ben is encouraging pupils to cross the playground by using a variety of large apparatus – tricycles, trikes and tractors. He places cones in strategic positions around the playground and invites the pupils to see what different routes they can make. Pupils with widely differing abilities and interests are fully engaged and appropriately challenged. Some choose to work independently whilst others prefer working with a group.

- In what other ways could Ben foster creative opportunities in this lesson?

Creativity is somewhat open-ended, as previously mentioned, in that it involves play in many contexts, including learning through play or playing with ideas, which could result in many different possibilities (NACCCE 1999). The curiosity of pupils can often bring about creative behaviour without their realizing that they are being creative. Teachers should be prepared for outcomes that may be very different from what they expect at the start, thus supporting a dynamic process. For example, a teacher could approach a topic creatively and encourage pupils to apply their imagination. By being engaged actively in a number of ways and using the raw material they have within them, they can create opportunities for themselves.

Reflective activity

Sue has planned for her Early Years class to explore the space around them. She has planned for the objectives to change as new ideas and possibilities present themselves. She starts with a simple game of tag which progresses and develops. She encourages the pupils to think of ideas of how they can change the game and she leads the pupils through the responses given. A range of tag games develop and progress to a very simple form of tag rugby.

- What other outcomes could have emerged as a result of exploring space?
- How has using pupils' intuition met the overall objectives of the lesson?

There needs to be a balance between teacher input and the understanding of the requirement to be free to innovate and take risks. This requires developing creative capacities such as the use of imagination and generation of many responses to a task. A teacher could experiment with alternatives and look for originality of response. For example, allowing pupils the opportunities to elaborate on current knowledge or skill and evaluation of processes and outcomes. These are all essential ingredients to creative learning.

Creative learning

Creative learning is possible across all elements of the National Curriculum and through all activity areas. Pupils' engagement in physical education can enhance both their mood and creativeness as a result of their quickening concentration and mental agility (Steinberg et al. 1997).

There are many opportunities for pupils to learn creatively. OfSTED (2010: 8) reported that creative learning was comprehended and fashioned by:

- questioning and challenging;
- making connections and seeing relationships;
- envisaging what might be;
- exploring ideas, keeping options open; and
- reflecting critically on ideas, actions and outcomes.

The primary school teacher can draw on these characteristics through different teaching styles (see Chapter 3) to promote learning. It is possible to inspire pupils to be free to express themselves and learn from their own and others' experiences. Taking responsibility for their own learning ought to be encouraged from Early Years schooling onwards. If pupils are placed in a creative environment in which they can learn creatively from the outset then they become open to further possibilities. For example, setting out a variety of indirect learning approaches allows pupils to select from a choice of responses (Rink 2002). This approach is significant in the Early Years, especially through imaginative play and learning through discovery, which aids the intellectual, social and emotional developmental processes (NACCCE 1999).

Example

Dan is teaching an Early Years class. He wants to promote self-directed learning and sets out to engage the pupils to look and listen in a constant process to devise their own games. He introduces a parachute and asks the pupils what they think they could do with it. The pupils are encouraged to respond both individually and in groups. The pupils think up names for their games. One pupil's idea is called the 'rainbow game' and the pupils decide they will try this game first. Using the colours of the parachute, Dan directs one pupil to start the game who does so by shouting out a colour. Those holding the parachute at the named colour have to run around the outside of the parachute and back to their place. The first pupil back shouts the name of the next colour.

- What strategies could Dan use to help the pupils to evaluate this game?

Linked with self- and peer assessment (see Chapter 5) pupils should be encouraged to monitor their own work and reflect upon their own and others' performance and progress. Allowing pupils to consider and pay due attention to their own thoughts, known as metacognition, gives rise to their taking ownership of their creativity. It hence helps them not just in their own development but also their sense of responsibility (NACCCE 1999). Allowing pupils the opportunity to think about their own thinking aids their creative learning. If this is coupled with bodily movement it helps them to become aware of their own creative and expressive actions. Pupils should have the scope for individual discovery in lessons. This may not always be apparent to them because the lessons are very well managed.

The diversity and range of physical activity allows many and varied opportunities for pupils to experience different forms of physical, emotional and social expression as well as an awareness of bodily actions and aesthetic appreciation. This is particularly the case for both dance and gymnastics.

Reflective activity

Maya is teaching gymnastics to Year Two. The theme is balance and she encourages the pupils to make a bridge. She asks the pupils to think and try out as many different shapes as they can – for example, long, hump-back, on their front and on their back. She encourages the pupils to think about their movements and to think what their movements feel like; she supports the pupils to let their ideas 'spin off'.

* How is Maya developing creativity with her pupils?

Reflective activity

For her Year Two class, Maya links the topic of dinosaurs to music and dance. For dance, she poses the questions, 'How do dinosaurs move?' and 'Can you think of different ways the dinosaur would travel?' She gets the pupils to use their imagination and to envisage large strides, strong movements and various speeds. The dance is composed of individual and group motifs and set against music they have pre-recorded using instruments which include drums and tambourines.

* How can Maya question the pupils to get them to think about how creative they have been?

Creativity is in itself a means of learning and according to NACCCE (1999) it has distinctive features:

- thoughtful playfulness, where learning occurs through experimental play and possibilities are explored and considered;
- the opportunity for individuals to challenge what they know and what they think they know, to help to learn afresh;
- the opportunity to seek out new possibilities to different situations in innovative fashion.

Creative learning and styles of learning in primary physical education need to be well planned and should be related to the skills, knowledge, understanding and evaluation of the National Curriculum. Creative learning is most effective when a controlled structure is provided which allows for flexible outcomes.

Reflective activity

Mark is teaching a games lesson to his Year Four class. He plans his lesson, which is structured and framed to give a certain degree of control and discipline but flexible enough to provide the freedom and confidence for pupils to experiment. His lesson is embedded in the National Curriculum and he aims for the pupils to plan, use and adapt strategies and tactics. Mark approaches the lesson by giving some guidance but is careful not to over-direct the pupils. The pupils' task is to invent an invasion game; they have to establish the aims of the game including methods of scoring, rules, roles and responsibilities. Mark encourages the pupils to evaluate their work and allow their ideas to develop over a period of time.

- How can Mark ensure that all pupils are challenged in this lesson?

It is possible that some pupils are denied the opportunity to develop their creative learning potential, especially if a lesson is too restrictive in its focus (OfSTED 2010) or if teachers fail to pick up and expand on pupils' ideas. Creative learning does involve commitment from the teacher and the school environment. In lessons, learning objectives do need to be clear, whilst simultaneously offering encouragement to pupils to make decisions, to investigate and reflect on progress made. Pupils ought to be given opportunities to experience creative learning as research indicates that:

- all young people have a wide range of abilities;
- these abilities are dynamically related and interactive;

- all pupils have strength in different areas of ability;
- success in one area can stimulate self-esteem and encourage success in others (NACCCE 1999: 66).

In addition, creativity is considered to be multidimensional, with different processes involving a variety of mental functions, combinations of skills and personality attributes which are all essential to creative learning. Creative learning is often a by-product of creative teaching.

Creative teaching

Different creative processes draw from a host of knowledge and practical skills, but to teach creatively teachers must draw from a number of strategies and imaginative approaches. Creative teaching aims to stimulate pupils' learning through exciting and effective lessons. A teacher can capture the interest and kindle the motivation of pupils by using good and effective teaching techniques. Teachers can be very creative in ways of getting pupils to learn, particularly if they know them well. Teachers need to have high expectations of themselves and of their pupils' abilities, as well as having the desire to help pupils develop their confidence and sense of self-belief. Creative teachers see opportunities for learning all the time.

Reflective activity

Catherine is teaching athletics to Year One with a focus on throwing. Catherine sets the scene and asks the pupils to picture themselves at the Olympic Games. She presents a range of equipment and instruments for measuring. She asks the pupils to make various selections from the full range of equipment and sets them different challenges. She encourages them to recognize and describe their actions using prompts such as 'What could you do to throw further?' 'What would happen if?' 'Can you change the action in any way?' 'How strong does the action make you feel?' The responses are discussed and the pupils are invited to select and try out the most successful techniques.

- What creative approach could Catherine take to develop these activities in follow-up lessons?

For creative teaching to be fully effective, it is important to develop a 'withitness' and know when to challenge learning, offer support or when to 'back off'.

It is important that feedback is provided and that a sense of balance is maintained. Questioning is an important feature of creative teaching, as illustrated in the above example. Questions should be well planned with the aim to facilitate creative thinking. Incorporating closed and open questions with the objective of creating many possible scenarios throughout a lesson can stimulate higher order thinking skills.

Reflective activity

Pupils in Donna's Year Six class are progressing in the game of netball. Donna considers that the pupils are improving in their passing skills and judges them to be ready for challenges regarding patterns of play and movement off the ball. Donna allows them the freedom to play but intervenes at key points during the games to pose several questions. She aims to foster a spirit of enquiry and brings to their attention a realization that there are multiple possibilities rather than one acceptable answer. Donna tries to promote their higher order thinking skills through analysis and synthesis, for example posing questions starting 'What if?' 'Why do you think?' 'What would happen if?' 'Can you compare what you did there to . . .?' 'What would you do differently?' and 'Why?'

- How should Donna approach asking the planned questions in this lesson?
- How can the class make best use of the responses given?

The remainder of this chapter will focus more closely on how the primary school teacher can use physical education to promote creative teaching and creative learning through teaching for creativity.

Teaching for creativity

Although some are of the opinion that creativity is a natural phenomenon that cannot be improved by education, others claim that creativity can be taught to pupils by encouraging their creative abilities (NACCCE 1999). A teacher has a responsibility to identify the creative capacities of a child and provide a suitable learning environment where potential can be nurtured and realized. Such a learning environment needs to take account of any planned formal teaching that may have a particular focus, for example the learning of a skill, but should be open enough to allow opportunities for experimentation, freedom of expression and creative development, whilst still allowing the skill to progressively develop.

In skill development or modelling any assessment criterion, teachers make frequent use of demonstrations. However, some teachers are wary that using demonstrations can stifle creativity, as noted by Rink (2002: 98–9), 'teachers who set creative responses, expressiveness, group projects, or problem solving processes as task goals are reluctant to use demonstrations in presenting the task'. The concern here is that some teachers may feel that demonstrations have the potential to impede pupils' impulses, which might be the case if only one possible outcome is presented to the pupils. Therefore, teaching for creativity involves a teacher teaching creatively to develop pupils' own creative thinking or behaviour. To be truly effective there needs to be a balance of both creative teaching and teaching for creativity.

Reflective activity

When teaching dance to Year Two, Sunita plays the music she wants the pupils to use for their movement. She asks them to lie down and close their eyes and concentrate on the music. As the music is playing she moves around the class and poses questions such as 'What does it make you think of?' 'How would you move?' Sunita questions the pupils and asks one pupil to demonstrate a given answer. Sunita sets the task of pupils working in pairs to make up a routine. The pupils are challenged to make connections between each other's ideas and present their ideas for peer review.

- What purpose did the demonstration serve in this lesson?
- Do you think using a demonstration in this way stifles creativity?

Pupils develop their creative capabilities if they are given the freedom to question, experiment and challenge and also the opportunity to express their own thoughts and ideas. A teacher needs to establish a creative environment that engages the creativity of both the teacher and pupils. Establishing such an atmosphere can be demanding and energy intensive but it is essential to motivate and inspire pupils.

Reflective activity

Simon is teaching dance to Year Six. He is working on the topic of time. The class is split into small groups and the groups are given props. A variety of old clocks and watches, which Simon has prepared for use by removing their backs or parts of their casings, are presented to each group. The groups are asked to investigate the props and write down what they see. They are encouraged to think of action words and to perform and work together as a team to represent a timepiece. They record their routines and work on musical arrangements to add to their performances.

- What does Simon need to do to ensure that there is a creative atmosphere for learning?

The NACCCE (1999) promoted three tasks that should be considered when teaching for creativity: encouraging, identifying and fostering. Based on the notion that those who are highly creative have a strong self-belief in what they are capable of, creativity in a child can be developed by a teacher who gives appropriate support and encouragement. Such encouragement in conjunction with motivation and a readiness to take risks can lead to opportunities for pupils to realize that they can succeed with a wealth of possibilities, which in turn gives them the confidence to have a go. Pupils can learn how to be determined and resilient if opportunities do not go to plan. In order for pupils to flourish creatively their potential abilities should be identified and subsequently fostered. Fostering the creativity in an individual child means developing aspects of their personality to the fullest, whilst accepting the diverse range of abilities and talents in a class (Cropley 2001). Teachers therefore need to provide an encouraging and supportive environment, be flexible in their approach, consider elements of experimentation and be prepared to try something different while being clear about their learning focus.

Reflective activity

In a Year Three athletics class, Julie presents a range of equipment to the pupils. She asks them to think about what the equipment could be used for and how it could be used. Julie sets out a lesson that fosters the curiosity of the pupils and provides appropriate imaginative activity. Using all the equipment, the pupils devise an obstacle course. There is a sense of excitement during the lesson as the pupils are prompted to envisage what might be possible. The pupils test the obstacle course and rate its effectiveness as a competition.

- What alternative outcomes are there for this lesson?

Reflective activity

Matt has been teaching the topic of the 'Egyptians' to Year Four and he wants to promote greater imagination and fluency from his pupils. He makes several cross-curricular connections, which the pupils understand and with which they are fully engaged; these include stories, paintings and sculptures of pyramids. He successfully fosters the enthusiasm of the pupils who are eager to turn their attention to an Egyptian dance which they devise by following a short teacher-led motif with imaginative group work.

- What should Matt take into consideration when fostering the enthusiasm of the pupils?

Teaching for creativity requires time and space. A teacher needs to give appropriate time for pupils to respond to a given situation, whether their response is via practical movement or thoughtful consideration of a question. There are occasions when time is required away from the task so that it can be revisited afresh. Suitable evaluation opportunities should be provided, which allow for reflection and constructive criticism in a non-threatening manner to make way for further development.

Reflective activity

In a Year One athletics lesson Sarah is teaching hurdles. She encourages the pupils to use all equipment available to them. When the pupils realize that there are no hurdles Sarah asks them to think about what they can use to create their own. The pupils work as a team and design and make their own hurdles using crates, poles, ropes and cones. They are fully engaged with the task and create differentiated heights to cater for the physical differences of pupils in the class without prompting. Sarah provides opportunities in the lesson to allow pupils to question, explore and challenge ideas.

- What strategies can Sarah incorporate to allow the pupils to think creatively?
- How can she support them to reflect on and evaluate their learning?

To cater for the different needs of pupils (see Chapter 4) a teacher ought to be aware that ideas may be generated in different ways and at different intervals.

All ideas should be allowed to be tested or at least talked through. Here the use of imagination, curiosity and questioning interplay.

Reflective activity

In a Year Three gymnastics lesson, Pat is teaching point and patch balances. She asks the pupils how many ways they can balance, particularly by using their hands and feet. She gets them to use their imagination to vary the balances by using different combinations. Pat encourages the pupils to think of questions they could ask one another on the success of the various balances.

- What guidance should Pat give to the pupils to help them pose their questions?

Reflective activity

In a Year Six short tennis lesson, Jade introduces the use of software analysis. Jade models basic ground strokes for the pupils to learn. As they practise the shots, they are able to evaluate their own performances by watching delayed video footage. The pupils are encouraged to seek solutions to improve their own level of skill but are also prompted to envisage alternative ways of correcting their mistakes. Jade realizes that although to learn certain skills, some aspects should be put in place, she also promotes pupil learning through independent enquiry.

- What strategies could Jade incorporate to encourage the pupils to engage in independent enquiry?

Reflective activity

Tom realizes that problem solving is not necessarily the same as creativity but he recognizes that pupils can find creative ways to come up with solutions to problems. He encourages the pupils in his Year Five class to think creatively when they are faced with problems set out for small teams. These include a 'spider's web', 'sheep in pens' and, when in the swimming pool, 'a raft race' (using big floats). Tom utilizes the varied nature of physical education and its challenging opportunities for pupils to develop their problem-solving abilities, creative thinking and communication and social skills. Tom is enthusiastic and makes effective use of creative approaches by promoting learning through a variety of connections. He maintains an open mind while the pupils explore a wide range of options and critically reflect on their ideas and outcomes.

- How much support should Tom give to pupils when they are engaged in problem-solving activities?
- How does Tom ensure all team members have the opportunity to contribute their ideas?

Summary

In summary, the aims of teaching for creativity incorporate a mutual trusting relationship between the teacher and child, which allows for respect and ownership with regard to the ideas that are being presented (Woods 1995; NACCCE 1999). This is achieved through a willingness to accept new and different ideas along with a variety of teaching approaches.

8 The use and abuse of ICT to enhance learning in physical education

Introduction

Although the provision of opportunities to apply and develop ICT capability is a current National Curriculum requirement in all subjects at Key Stage 2, several recently published guides to primary physical education make virtually no reference at all to ICT and specific research in this field is scarce. However, the centrality of ICT, not only as an area of learning in its own right, but also as one that should be embedded in the teaching of all subjects, is endorsed by both the *Rose Report* (Rose 2009) and the *Cambridge Primary Review* (Alexander 2009). The potential of ICT to contribute to enhancing learning in physical education will be a key focus of this chapter and some of the pitfalls of misusing ICT will also be highlighted. The effective use of a range of technologies will be illustrated through examples of good practice, such as the use of data recording software to log individual performances in athletics or the use of camcorders and digital cameras to analyse and improve dance or gymnastics work. Reflective questions will be posed to encourage critical analysis of the value of specific ICT uses within the physical education context.

Curriculum opportunities

Information and communication technology opportunities are highlighted in the National Curriculum for physical education (year 2000 version) for Key Stages 1 and 2 whereby suggestions are made as to how ICT can be incorporated in the programme of study (DfEE/QCA 1999). These suggestions include the use of video and CD-ROMs to view and record movement and actions to help pupils to evaluate performances and develop their ideas, as well as using a concept keyboard to record the order of specific actions in their sequences. These technologies can be adapted and applied in many different contexts to any of the activities taught. It is most likely that ICT will have the potential to contribute to learning in physical education irrespective of the detail of future curricula. It is worth bearing in mind that available technologies advance quickly and gadgets and documentation date rapidly, so a teacher needs to be open to new developments and be flexible and creative when approaching teaching and learning with ICT in physical education, as will be explained later in the chapter.

Reflective activity

Paul shows his Year Four class a short video clip of a factory run by machines, which he has set to music. He asks the pupils to describe the movements the machines make. He also refers to the music to encourage the pupils to recognize and feel the rhythm. He uses the video and music as stimuli for a class dance. The pupils work in pairs and small groups and produce machine-type movements using the same music. The final class performance is video recorded and the pupils evaluate their own and others' work. They also compare and contrast their performance with the original video footage.

- How does the use of ICT impact on the learning experience of the pupils?
- How could this approach to teaching dance be incorporated into other activity areas?

Range of technologies

The range of available technologies for teaching and learning is vast, including, among others, camcorders, digital cameras, data recording software (for example spreadsheets), analysis software, the Internet, laptops or palmtops, CD-ROMs or DVDs, heart monitors and stopwatches. The more appropriate opportunities pupils have to access such equipment, the greater their prospects for learning. However, there is much more to consider than simply being exposed to equipment. The resources must be used for the purposes of improving learning, often by building on what has gone before but in a deeper more meaningful, creative and powerful way. The applied use of technology can contribute to nurturing pupils' cognitive skills in a profound fashion. For example, in a swimming lesson where the pupils are practising their back crawl, the teacher can incorporate software analysis in the lesson. The use of software analysis can assist the pupils in their learning by helping them to think about the movements that they are making. By watching delayed playback of their performances on a split screen alongside a demonstration of a swimmer showing the 'perfect' stroke the pupils gain a deeper understanding of what they are aiming for.

There are different stages of using and engaging with ICT to enhance learning in physical education. Like questioning, ICT can be embraced at lower, middle and higher orders of thinking and engagement (Bloom 1956) (see Chapter 5).

Reflective activity

Lower order

Caitlin is introducing her Year Three class to the game of netball. She sets the pupils the task of finding out about the game using the Internet. She asks them to recall and report the information to check their knowledge and understanding.

Middle order

During small-sided game play the pupils have to rotate in after five minutes of play which they monitor via a stopwatch. During their time off court the pupils apply their knowledge and complete worksheets to examine others' performances.

Higher order

The pupils watch video footage of a variety of passes selected by Caitlin; she also produces task cards outlining the key learning points. Through play, the pupils have to monitor their own development and improvement of their own and others' skills. They analyse the performances and are asked to make distinctions between good and poor passes.

- How do you decide if the planned ICT is the most appropriate for the lesson?
- What factors do you take into consideration when deciding how pupils can access, select and interpret the information to enhance their knowledge and understanding?

In addition to the equipment mentioned thus far, the range of multimedia to support learning is extensive including the use of electronic dance mats, digital pets where pupils can learn about health and wellbeing, as well as commercial software packages that are geared towards improvement in pupils' subject knowledge. The latter are often targeted towards cross-curricular themes.

Reflective activity

Maggie is addressing knowledge and understanding of fitness and health with her Year Five pupils. She engages the pupils in a cross-curricular project focusing particularly on physical education, science and mathematics.

She is teaching the pupils how exercise affects the body in the short term and why physical activity is good for health and wellbeing. Maggie devises a 'cross-country' route around the school grounds; the route involves many changes of direction due to restricted outdoor space. Maggie splits the class into similar ability groups and the groups run the route in relay legs. They are responsible for a collective time which they measure using a stopwatch and they each wear a pedometer. The pedometer records their steps and distance travelled and the pupils are guided how to pace each leg of the relay. After the relay, the pupils return to the classroom and design a spreadsheet and plot their data.

Linked to their mathematics lessons they work with different systems to record their data and, coupled with science, they learn about how the heart pumps blood around the body. Computer images of this lead to engagement and greater understanding.

- What opportunities are provided for pupils to assess their learning?
- What targets ought to be set to further challenge the pupils?

Teachers can also make good use of their school's websites and intranets to promote learning through support and enhancement in physical education as well as developing their virtual learning environments. Work in physical education could be showcased on a school's website or via links to a secure section of the site. As part of reflection activity, based on their practical work, the pupils could add weekly 'blogs' as well as downloading material and displaying video footage. This could also be connected to an online reporting system, thus promoting parental involvement and strengthening a school's link to homes.

Links to home

Technology in the home has significantly increased in recent years and continues as an upward trend. This undoubtedly affects how pupils respond to technological equipment in school, although it should be recognized that some pupils will have greater access and richer experiences than others who may well be disadvantaged. It is probably beneficial to audit what access the pupils have to aid differentiated learning experiences. For example, from very young ages some pupils are familiar with social online games and networking sites. Many have their own mobile phones and communicate by text, gather information through search engines or Wikipedia, as well as downloading games, music and films (Alexander 2009). Even though pupils are exposed to such a variety of technology at home, it remains the role of the teacher to harness its learning potential.

Using ICT to enhance teaching and learning

OfSTED (2009b) reported examples of effective uses of ICT, claiming that it had a positive impact on the wellbeing and personal development of pupils (see Chapter 2), as well as contributing significantly towards their ability to work both independently and cooperatively. Indeed, ICT has the potential to promote and aid the development of pupils' capacity to take ownership of their work and plan future pathways (DfEE/QCA 1999). This can enthuse them and boost their motivation. However, using ICT to enhance teaching and learning needs to be properly planned, appropriate and focused to support pupil activity. Pupils need to be given opportunities to engage with ICT in order for it to support their learning fully. By the end of Year Six they should be able to find and select information from a variety of digital sources including using the Internet and be able to work with the information. For example, they should be able to make a judgement about what is reliable and accurate. They should develop their digital literacy and be able to engage with a range of multimedia, by accessing information that allows them to work with sound, vision (still and moving pictures) and text. They should be able not only to create work but to communicate ideas to their peers and adults on a one-to-one basis or to an audience. Whilst the work that pupils do in physical education contributes to improving their study skills across other curriculum areas, physical education provides unique opportunities to offer different ICT experiences essential to preparing them for their future.

Computer-based work was a major feature of the OfSTED (2009b) report on good practice where they found pupils demonstrating their ability to work both independently and collaboratively whilst diligently responding to the teacher's instructions. Parallels with these findings from inspections were noted by Alexander (2009) in the *Cambridge Primary Review*, who concluded that there needed to be balanced connections between periods of pupil independent modes of learning and the guided tuition of the teacher.

Such guidance relies on characteristics of good teaching (see Chapters 3, 5 and 7), for example modelling, questioning and supportive feedback. The use of carefully selected resources can aid pupils' motivation to learn and can also contribute to their eye-limb coordination. This is especially the case if ICT work is embedded throughout the primary phases with planned development building from Early Years to Year Six. Pupils in primary education are capable of a range of skills including data handling, presentation and working with multimedia. They are capable of using ICT well for communicating their ideas, where communicating is much more than speaking and listening (Alexander 2009).

Reflective activity

The pupils have been working on a cross-curricular topic of dance from other countries. They have learnt existing dances as well as devising their own, which they have practised and performed at their own dance festival for family, friends and the community. All age groups in the school have participated and have contributed to a visual display alongside the physical performances. The display encapsulates eye-catching designs, poems and still photographs.

- How can ICT opportunities be utilized to follow up activities to this event?

Work with ICT in physical education can contribute to raising standards in literacy, thus pupils can engage with the vocabulary for physical education. For example, pupils can devise their own instructional task cards, which include images sourced from the Internet, or make their own instructional videos. These examples can capture the pupils' interest and promote their learning. Information and communication technology can also be beneficial when catering for pupils who have English as an additional language to aid their construction of sentences, as well as helping pupils with learning difficulties and/or disabilities (see Chapter 4).

Reflective activity

Debbie found her teaching role challenging when new pupils joined her Year One class whose command of English was very poor. Debbie incorporated lots of demonstration in her lessons but she found working with images she had sourced from the Internet and using photographs of other pupils' work coupled with key words printed on cards to be very helpful. The ICT resources helped to ease the frustration felt by pupils and assisted them in their learning of the English language.

- What other resources could aid teaching pupils with EAL?
- How could the approach outlined in this study be developed in the pupils' future work?
- How could other pupils work with pupils with EAL?

Planning is essential for the successful implementation of ICT in physical education lessons. To ensure quality, a teacher should address how pupils can progress and develop their ICT skills, integrated with their knowledge and understanding in different contexts (OfSTED 2009b). In addition, planning requires that the full range of pupils' needs, from those needing additional support to those of high attainment, are met. This is particularly important as ICT has the potential to develop critical, creative and more complex thinking (Alexander 2009). So, once the lesson is planned, teaching should take into account how it can be implemented systematically and intelligently. A teacher needs to recognize the limitations of ICT, or face the pitfalls that this can bring (National Association for Advisors for Computers in Education 2007). These are covered in more detail in due course.

Reflective activity

Emily is finding teaching gymnastics to her Year Six class a challenge due to the variation in the pupils' ability. In focusing on sequence work, Emily needs to differentiate the learning objectives to meet the pupils' individual needs. Emily produces task cards (word-processed with clear pictures) to assist her teaching. This provides a visual stimulus for the pupils so that all can work at their own pace and be actively involved in self- and peer assessment, whilst at the same time being appropriately challenged.

- How does a teacher differentiate to meet the full range of learning?
- What aspects of ICT could assist in the differentiated teaching of this class?

The working environment is an important issue to consider when planning lessons for ICT in physical education. Whilst some activities may be computer-based, at a fixed location such as a computer room, others may be at a variety of venues such as a classroom, the school hall, playing fields, yard, gym or pool. The teacher needs a flexible and adaptable approach. For example, using waterproof casings for hand-held cameras on the poolside or in the water and laptops or electronic notebooks with wireless Internet access strategically placed in a hall or outdoors.

Example

At the Year Five outdoor and adventurous activity residential camp, Grant splits the class into small groups. He issues each group with a 'flip' camera to make short recordings of the activities they have undertaken. Each evening the groups download their footage onto a laptop and collaboratively produce a diary, taking turns to word-process their experiences. In follow-up lessons the pupils take turns to present their diaries to the rest of the class.

Example

Kay takes her class of Year One pupils to their first of a series of swimming lessons. The ability of the pupils in the class ranges from those who can swim a recognized stroke unaided to those who are complete beginners, who lack water confidence. Kay takes along some simple mini-lightweight handheld cameras, which she has inserted in waterproof casings. She encourages the non-swimmers to put their heads under the water by asking the pupils to film footage of objects she has strategically placed on the pool floor. The pupils are so engaged in the activity that they quickly gain water confidence.

- How could this equipment be used to challenge the learning of more able pupils?
- What other ICT resources can be incorporated into the teaching of swimming?
- What issues ought a teacher to consider when using electronic technology on the poolside?

The use of projectors and interactive whiteboards can also help facilitate learning. If teaching assistants are available, it is important that they are considered and consulted at the planning stage. An additional adult can be an asset to pupils' learning if appropriately engaged in the lesson.

Example

Paul finds that using his interactive whiteboard helps his Year Six class to grasp a better understanding of the practical activities that they are undertaking. He encourages the pupils to use the board in many ways, including using templates so they can plot their positions, roles and responsibilities in games, plan the layout of apparatus in gymnastics and share data obtained in athletics.

Reflective activity

Teaching a gymnastics lesson to Year Four, Sandeep is working on the theme of individual travel with an emphasis on variation of speed, changes in direction, the pathways taken and pause. The pupils take turns to video record the work; the recording is taken from the same angle for all the pupils. The teaching assistant helps the teacher in their usual way of clarifying the learning objectives and learning points but also takes video footage at the same time as the pupils but from a different position. Pupils have the opportunity to view their work from different angles on a split-screen playback.

•   What aspects of evaluation would this approach contribute to?
•   In what other ways could the teaching assistant be employed to promote learning with ICT?

Whilst ICT has the potential to contribute to enhancing learning in physical education there are also potential drawbacks to consider.

Implications of using ICT in physical education lessons

One of the many pitfalls of working with technology is that it sometimes fails to work and teachers need to be able to adapt in such circumstances. It might be the case that a technician can offer support but if such help is not available it is important that a teacher does not shy away from experimenting or trying something new. It may be the case that the pupils themselves are trained to support each other and the teacher; as OfSTED (2009b) found, pupils operating in this role were very keen individuals who took their responsibilities seriously.

Like all good physical education teaching, for ICT to make a difference to pupils' learning it is important that it is given the time and space. There is little point in 'doing it, for the sake of doing it' or treating it as an 'add or bolt on' in order to 'tick a box'. This is sometimes the case when there has been investment in resources that a teacher fails to utilize, or that a teacher uses to aid teaching but neglects to fully embed in the potential learning, as the following reflective activity illustrates.

Reflective activity

Richard is teaching athletics to his Early Years class. The pupils are developing their running techniques. Richard shares the objectives for the lesson, sets the tasks for the pupils and then spends the majority of the lesson filming the pupils with a handheld video camera.

- How far has the use of ICT impacted on the pupils' learning?
- What improvements could be made to enhance learning through the use of the video camera?
- What opportunities are there for pupils to have 'hands-on' experience?

Teachers need to have high expectations and continually aim to challenge their pupils. As OfSTED (2009b) found, many ineffective lessons were the result of teachers' expectations being too low. The resulting slow-paced lessons resulted in pupils securing what they already knew instead of developing their higher level skills. This failed to motivate pupils or to promote creativity and stifled their independence. It also failed to promote their ability to evaluate, review or share their work with others. OfSTED (2009b) claim that it is particularly towards the end of Key Stage 2, where pupil progress slows, which can negate gains from previous years.

Where the focus is more on teaching and less on learning, the consequences often lead to limited question opportunities. It is more a case of checking whether pupils have understood what they were asked to do rather than extending and assessing their specific understanding of ICT in physical education. Therefore, even if teachers can use ICT to improve their teaching, they still need to consider how they address issues of learning. They need to develop their knowledge and skills to engage pupils fully in the learning process. Secure subject knowledge is required in both ICT and physical education if learning is to be maximized.

Aspects of effective assessment in relation to learning in ICT and physical education will be considered in due course. It is the ineffective assessment that adds to the pitfalls of using ICT, the biggest criticism being that teachers fail to track their pupils' progress sufficiently. In addition, there can be missed opportunities for pupils to engage in peer and self-assessment, which is perhaps poor practice given that many of the resources available are intended to enhance assessment for learning. Indeed, OfSTED (2009b) reported assessment was the weakest feature of teaching for ICT – it was adequate in only one school in five.

Pupils' progression in different aspects of ICT ought to be monitored. For example, they may be proficient in using ICT to communicate ideas but they need more guidance in the use of data logging and spreadsheets. It would help if pupils could be provided with further experiences to link their practical and theoretical work. However, it can be difficult to maintain a balance of activities given the very practical nature of physical education. Nonetheless, if pupils are only exposed to a narrow range of learning opportunities or applications to choose from, progress will remain limited.

As with all other subjects in the curriculum, when engaging with learning that incorporates email and Internet use for physical education lessons, teachers have to embed safety in all activities (DfES 2003a). For example, pupils need to be taught not to disclose personal details and to learn how to deal with potential dangers. There are issues with too much exposure to electronic equipment, which include accessing unmonitored websites and the 'adverse consequences to pupils' physical health and social development of spending long solitary hours at the computer screen and by the addictive nature of computer games' (Alexander 2009: 226).

It ought to be recognized that while some schools have access to a wealth of resources, others are more limited. Teachers need to modify and be creative in what they can do where resources are scarce. However, as previously mentioned, teachers do need to keep abreast of future developments in technology and the opportunities they bring to improve teaching and learning. Indeed, the technological equipment, particularly games, that pupils have access to in their homes mean that some pupils' awareness and capability far exceeds that of their teachers. In these instances it is possible that pupils do not always make sufficient progress, which can lead to underachievement (OfSTED 2009b) and hence suppress their motivation.

Assessment of ICT to support teaching and learning in physical education

Assessment of teaching and learning incorporating ICT tends to follow the national pattern for assessment in other aspects of physical education (see Chapter 5). Pupils should be encouraged to create informative portfolios of their work. These should be integrated and measured against the learning objectives and show what they have achieved as well as identifying areas for improvement.

Assessment is strong when planning is detailed and thorough, with meticulous attention paid to inform the next stages of learning. Teachers should apply assessment strategies to ICT as they would any other aspect of physical education. For example, using effective and timely feedback, tracking progress and allowing pupils the opportunity to self- and peer assess will fully engage pupils in their own learning. Teachers should ask challenging questions skilfully to assess pupils' understanding and to close gaps and build on their knowledge. Teachers need to be consistent in their approaches to assessment of ICT and a portfolio of work can contribute towards monitoring pupils who are on track, working above or below their expected outcomes and thus aid their future challenge.

Reflective activity

Year Six pupils are working on performing actions and skills with more consistent control and quality; they are working on gymnastic sequences in pairs. Becky, their teacher, issues a 'flip' camera to each group and they each have access to a laptop; the pupils are encouraged to complete the task and improve their own performances with the aid of the ICT equipment throughout the lesson. During the plenary the pupils evaluate their own and others' work against the learning objectives.

- How has the use of ICT on this occasion contributed to pupil learning?
- How should the teacher track and monitor the progress made by individuals?

Summary

Overall, as illustrated throughout this chapter, it is possible to provide significant opportunities to incorporate ICT in the teaching of primary physical education. The chapter has demonstrated that ICT can provide:

- a stimulus to activity, for example videos to initiate work in dance or the use of electronic dance mats;
- feedback, for instance using heart monitors to inform about the impact of exercise or cameras to provide images of performances;
- tools for analysis, such as data analysis software or software for analysing movement;
- information, for example through video images of correct techniques;

- resources to support inclusive learning, including photographs, task cards or other images for pupils with language difficulties;
- information sharing, by using podcasts or video conferencing.

Purposeful ICT opportunities can enthuse and motivate pupils, maximizing their attainment and encouraging them to become independent learners. Creative use of ICT can also help address issues such as the implementation of differentiation activities.

9 Sites for learning: the outdoor classroom

Introduction

Outdoor education has played an important part in British education for many years. The 1990 physical education National Curriculum included the recommendation that all pupils should be entitled to a residential outdoor and adventurous experience. This recognition of the value of residential stays dates back to the 1944 Education Act in which the proposal for a period of residence in the country was based on a concern for pupils' health (Humberstone 1992). 'Outdoor and adventurous activities' (OAA) have been included as a physical education activity area in every version of the primary National Curriculum although the current model does not include OAA until Key Stage 2. The reality has been that many schools have chosen activity areas other than OAA because of a lack of confidence in teachers' abilities to deliver these activities and because of concerns about health and safety. In 2004 OfSTED noted that lack of teacher confidence prevented teachers from fully exploiting outdoor learning opportunities (OfSTED 2004). Some teachers tend to assume that OAA refer to activities such as canoeing, sailing, rock climbing and mountaineering, which are clearly beyond the capabilities of the generalist and, indeed, of most physical education specialists. The reality is that there is great potential for introducing pupils to OAA within the school grounds or the immediate locality and that are not high risk. Orienteering-based activities or cooperative and trust-building activities not only achieve the purposes of outdoor activities within the physical education context but also have considerable cross-curricular potential. These form the basis of OAA for Key Stage 2 pupils within the most recent version of the National Curriculum.

While OAA does not feature within the National Curriculum for Key Stage 1 or the Foundation Stage, the importance of links between education and the outdoor environment, both within the school boundaries and further afield, has received growing recognition. The importance of outdoor play and its potential as a vehicle for learning should not be underestimated given the significance attached to planned, purposeful play within the Early Years Foundation Stage statutory framework (DCSF 2008a).

> Young children in the Foundation Stage moved independently from indoors to outdoors staying with their own choice of activity. They were used to this free-flow which enabled them to use their imagination and pursue their ideas with autonomy. It also helped them to develop their understanding of staying safe.
>
> (OfSTED 2008a: 13)

Outdoor learning is a more recent and broader concept embracing a range of locations, including school grounds, parks, playing fields, outdoor centres and other local facilities. It encompasses a wide range of learning outcomes across different subject areas as well as personal, social and emotional aspects of learning. It includes activities such as mountaineering which can only be taught and learned in an outdoor setting and others, such as map-reading skills, that can be undertaken in the classroom but that will be enhanced by being located outdoors. It is based on a recognition that many different aspects of the National Curriculum can be taught through judicious use of the outdoors. Following the publication of *Excellence and Enjoyment* (DfES 2003b) with its emphasis on learning that is 'exciting and engaging' for pupils (DfES 2003b: 1) plus reviews of the primary curriculum (Rose 2009; Alexander 2009) with a focus on reducing the amount of prescription within the curriculum, foundations are in place for the further development of the potential of the outdoors as a learning environment. This is, however, likely to depend upon the commitment of the individual school and teachers. Specific outdoor learning opportunities are provided by initiatives such as Forest Schools (Knight 2009). Several of the Foundation Stage physical development outcomes can be achieved using outdoor learning activities incorporating other benefits including those related to personal and social development.

Residential experiences remain highly desirable with enormous potential for learning related both to aspects of physical education and to a whole range of broader aims. Not only do pupils benefit from the personal and social learning that accrues from the residential element but there is also the potential, given a carefully chosen centre, for an introduction to a range of activities that cannot be provided by school staff.

This chapter will review the nature and benefits of outdoor learning as well as discussing some of the barriers. It will describe some specific examples of outdoor learning initiatives to illustrate the possibilities open to the primary school teacher.

Sites for outdoor learning

Outdoor learning can take place in a wide range of environments, some of which are more accessible than others (DfES 2006). These include:

School grounds

School grounds offer opportunities for formal and informal learning and for play. They have the potential to provide a rich resource for all schools, including adventure play equipment, woodland areas, gardens or planting areas, story telling or quiet areas, different kinds of habitat (meadows, ponds, playing fields) and orienteering areas:

> Children in the reception class at Chawson First School in Droitwich arrive at school one day every week dressed in old clothes. Come rain or shine they have time outdoors. A sample of the experiences include building shelters, running to find a leaf longer than . . ., making a trap to catch a dinosaur (using ropes and logs), planting bulbs and seeds, digging, a range of activities using balls and hoops . . . Forest School has been so successful that it is now part of the Year One curriculum.
>
> (CfSA 2009)

Local environment

This refers to the immediate local environment within walking distance of the school. The local environment provides opportunities to enrich a range of curriculum areas through exploration of the locality. Specific activities will depend on the location which might include heritage sites, sites of special scientific interest, city farms, parks and woodland, land and streetscapes, arts venues and activity trails.

Example

Year Four works in groups designing community trails to show places of interest in their immediate locality. They select ten stopping places that reflect the area, such as old buildings, interesting features such as letter boxes, statues or signs, churches, local information centres. Each group produces a map of its trail with instructions about how to go from one point to the next and information about each stopping point.

Places further afield

These can provide contrasts with the immediate locality, with further learning opportunities. They might include museums, field study or environment centres, activity centres, science parks, theatre workshops, country or national parks, nature reserves, zoos and aquaria or farms and gardens.

Residential locations

The benefits of residential experiences have long been recognized. These include outdoor activity centres, field study centres, cultural visits in the UK or abroad and summer camps or expeditions:

> I remember a lot of good things about my week at Outward Bound, like building a shelter with my friend Alice and cooking bread sticks over an open fire with Emma our instructor. But I especially remember the big mountain I climbed – I've not done that before and I was scared of heights. When I stood at the bottom of the mountain and looked up it felt so high. But when I got to the top and looked down it no longer felt so high. I was very proud and happy to have climbed it (Claire, 10).
>
> (Outward Bound Trust 2010)

> Every year, Year Five embarks on a residential educational visit to Llandudno where they undertake activities reaching across many topic areas and providing both immediate learning and ones that help them develop throughout the year. Students gained first hand experiences that bolstered their understanding in specific subjects such as history and geography whilst also developing their presentational and personal independence skills.
>
> (LOTC 2008)

Benefits of outdoor learning

Outdoor learning has been endorsed for many years for its ability to provide challenge, managed risk and opportunities for personal and social development. Its potential contribution to the development of personal and social skills was noted by David Bell, Her Majesty's Chief Inspector in 2004:

> Outdoor activities both at school and on residential courses enable pupils to enjoy challenging and unfamiliar experiences that test and

develop their physical, personal and social skills. They can be the most memorable experiences for pupils of their school days.

One longstanding provider of outdoor activities is the Outward Bound Trust, which provides a range of opportunities at various centres, including courses for older primary school pupils. One school comments:

> It's hard to pin down the huge benefits of the Outward Bound experience as it impacts on the pupils in so many ways. It builds teamwork, confidence, flexibility, responsiveness to challenges and an appreciation of nature and the wider world.
>
> (Outward Bound Trust 2010)

A more recent focus has been on the potential of outdoor learning to impact positively on learning and achievement. The DfES (2006) suggests that outdoor education can provide a bridge between theory and reality and improve attitudes to learning through stimulating, inspiring and motivating. Their view is supported by Dismore who presents evidence to suggest that outdoor education can have a positive effect on motivation and engagement in learning and on achievement (Dismore and Bailey 2005). This may be through making learning more relevant and engaging, thereby deepening and enriching it (DfES 2006). OfSTED (2008a) also claims that the first-hand experiences of learning outside the classroom can help make subjects more vivid and interesting for pupils and enhance their understanding and thus can help combat underachievement. Learners of all ages involved in the survey said that they enjoyed working away from the classroom. Outdoor education provides many opportunities for informal learning through play (DfES 2006). The importance of informal learning is emphasized by Rea (2008) who suggests that the strength of outdoor centres lies in their ability to maximize opportunities for, and to capitalize on, informal learning.

For young children, regular outdoor experiences are thought to not only promote physical development but also to affect cognitive, creative and social development. Parsons (2006) claims that providing Foundation Stage children with more stimulating outdoor opportunities contributes towards their physical, cognitive, social, creative and emotional development. OfSTED provides evidence in support of this view.

> A visit to a farm proved to be a highly stimulating experience for one Reception class. Two weeks later, when the inspector visited, children were still talking enthusiastically about what they had seen and done. They were also proud to show the writing that they had produced about the farm. This was of a better standard than might be expected

from pupils of their age, but, more importantly, a stark improvement
on the writing that they had done before the visit.

(OfSTED 2008a: 10)

The English Outdoor Council suggests that outcomes of high-quality
outdoor education should include:

- enjoyment and a positive attitude to challenge and adventure;
- personal confidence and self-esteem;
- self-awareness and social skills and an appreciation of the contributions and achievements of themselves and others;
- appreciation of the natural environment and an understanding of the
  importance of conservation and sustainable development;
- a range of skills in outdoor activities, expeditions and exploration;
- increased initiative, reliance, responsibility, perseverance and
  commitment;
- development and extension of skills of communication, problem
  solving, leadership and teamwork;
- appreciation of the benefits of physical fitness and lifelong participation in healthy leisure activities;
- motivation and appetite for learning contributing to raised levels of
  attainment in other areas of the curriculum;
- broadened horizons leading to a wider range of employment opportunities and life chances (Outdoor Education Advisers Panel 2005: 8).

These outcomes resonate with the OfSTED (2008a) conclusion that
outdoor learning can contribute significantly to pupils' personal, social and
emotional development.

A year after the Outdoor Education Council's publication, the Outdoor
Learning Manifesto suggested an overlapping range of benefits, subject to
good planning, safe management and personalization to the needs of the
individual:

- improve academic achievement;
- provide a bridge to higher order learning;
- develop skills and independence in a widening range of environments;
- make learning more engaging and relevant to young people;
- develop active citizens and stewards of the environment;
- nurture creativity;
- provide opportunities for informal learning through play;
- reduce behaviour problems and improve attendance;
- stimulate, inspire and improve motivation;
- develop the ability to deal with uncertainty;

- provide challenge and the opportunity to take acceptable levels of risk;
- improve young people's attitude to learning (DfES 2006: 4).

Both link clearly to key areas of the *Every Child Matters* agenda – namely, enjoying and achieving, staying safe and being healthy (DfES 2003a).

Approaches to outdoor learning

Cooper (1998) suggests that the outdoors can be used in different ways in order to promote learning. These include:

- Adventurous activities – focusing on physical skills, on personal, social and environmental awareness, or on potential leisure activities, and including activities such as orienteering, mountaineering, canoeing, sailing and climbing. These clearly fall within the remit of physical education.
- Field studies – often related to other subjects such as geography or science and including investigative skills and practical activities.
- Problem solving – usually with a focus on specific personal, social or team-building skills using group activities.
- Aesthetic and environmental awareness – involving using the outdoors as a stimulus for a personal response that may include sensory activities, writing, drawing, dance or drama.
- Practical conservation – using practical skills in projects related to the improvement of the environment.

Active learning or learning by doing is key to learning outdoors.

Outdoor learning and physical education

Within the broader concept of outdoor learning, there are a number of elements that have particular relevance in the context of physical education and physical activity.

OAA comprise one of the activity areas in the National Curriculum through which the aims of physical education are achieved. While the current National Curriculum includes OAA as an activity area at Key Stage 2, the benefits of outdoor learning are equally apparent at Key Stage 1 and the Foundation Stage. Outdoor and adventurous activities include activities that can be taught within the immediate locality by the class teacher as well as by specialist staff at offsite locations. Norfolk County Council offers the following rationale for choosing to deliver physical education through OAA.

Outdoor and adventurous activities should provide:

- an exciting medium through which to stimulate and reinforce learning;
- a powerful vehicle through which to address objectives in personal and social education;
- a variety of physical activities, chiefly non-competitive, which offer alternative avenues for pupil achievement and attainment;
- an encouragement to young people to adopt a healthy lifestyle based on an enjoyment and appreciation of the outdoors (Norfolk County Council 2010).

The aims of high-quality OAA can be summarized as:

- To introduce children to different environments.
- To explore other areas of the curriculum through the medium of OAA.
- To give children strategies for developing personal skills and interests.
- To give children the opportunity to learn through fun and challenging learning activities.
- To develop positive attitudes and behaviour in children.
- To build upon qualities of sharing, working together and developing ways of communicating.
- To give opportunities to develop leadership skills (Norfolk County Council 2010).

While some OAA clearly require specialist facilities and staffing, many activities can be taught by the non-specialist teacher, within school grounds and with no specialized equipment. Many of these activities are based on orienteering and navigation activities or on problem-solving and trust activities and are the focus of OAA within the National Curriculum at Key Stage 2. For example:

- In OAA as a whole, pupils follow maps and trails, try to solve physical problems and challenges, and learn how to work safely in a range of situations.
- In Year Three pupils take part in simple orientation activities using maps and diagrams. They are set physical challenges and problems to solve, and work on their own and in small groups.

- In Year Four pupils learn how to read and follow different maps and symbol trails. They also take part in a range of trust and communication activities, and in some adventure games.
- In Years Five/Six pupils develop their orienteering and problem-solving skills in familiar and unfamiliar situations and environments. Throughout, there is an emphasis on building trust and working as a team (QCDA 2000).

Example

Year Two are working on a 'Follow that picture' challenge. They work in pairs and follow a trail that uses pictures and photos of features around the school grounds, including soccer goalposts, a picnic table, a beech tree and specific playground markings. At each point there is information that has to be collected, for example labels tell them, in words and pictures, the number of goals scored during the season in soccer matches, the constituent parts of a healthy picnic and the age of the beech tree. There are three time bands within an overall time limit for which pairs can gain gold, silver or bronze provided that they have collected all the pieces of information. (This activity promotes cooperative working, recognition of how the body feels during exercise, successful travel to different locations and exploration of school grounds and surroundings.)

As Robertson (1994) points out, OAA in the primary school does not require pupils to take part in the whole range of outdoor pursuits such as canoeing, rock climbing, sailing or mountaineering. However, evidence from pupils who have had the opportunity to take part in activity days or residential experiences demonstrates the power of such activities as a learning medium where schools are able to access facilities and specialist teaching. For example, 'I didn't think I'd be able to do the climbing. When I managed it I thought, "You've just got to believe you can do something"' (Dismore and Bailey 2005).

Trust-based or problem-solving activities have the potential to combine physical activity with team-building exercises and activities that have a sensory element.

Example

Touch Hunt is a scavenger hunt in which participants are asked to find and collect half a dozen natural 'touches'. The list should encourage pupils to pick and feel natural objects and choose one that fits the description well. Objects could include something 'crunchy', something 'bendy', something 'rough', something 'sticky', something 'tickly' and something 'cold'. Pupils work in groups and share their touches to select an 'exhibition' of the ones that they see as the best representatives of each category. The exhibition is labelled and presented to other groups. This activity is physically active and involves group work, language work, sensory input and communication. (Example adapted from Cooper 1998)

Example

About 12 people form a caterpillar joining in a line, holding onto each other's waists. Each becomes a segment of the caterpillar and all are blindfolded except the front person who is the head of the caterpillar. The caterpillar follows a route that may go through bushes, over logs and under branches with the head directing the group using verbal instructions. The head can change so that all have the opportunity to lead. A further challenge is to ask the group to find a form of non-verbal communication to move the caterpillar along a prescribed route. Reviewing the activity should enable groups to identify key qualities needed for success, namely communication, trust and cooperation. (Adapted from Cooper 1998)

Much informal learning can take place in the outdoor setting of the playground. It also offers many opportunities for physical activity, which contributes towards the development of healthy lifestyles. Several of these are discussed in Chapter 4 and others have been developed as part of the PESSCL and PESSYP initiatives. These recommend the development of spaces outdoors where physical activity can be used to develop learning in other subjects at breaks and lunchtimes. Structured purposeful physical activities can also promote team work, cooperation and listening skills. The example below has created the potential for pupils to develop their understanding, through informal though structured activity, in a range of physical activities including dance as well as both individual and team games.

Example

Fair Furlong audited pupil needs and then established areas for a range of different pupil activities in the playground including:

- areas for quiet activities with good-quality seating and board games;
- a fenced ball park for fast-flowing mini-sports;
- areas for more general physical activity such as basketball shooting, kingball, catch-up and 'piggy in the middle'.

The school also invested in good-quality physical education equipment for use exclusively at playtimes and lunchtimes, including a dance stage with music where pupils could develop their own dance routines.

After- or out-of-school clubs also give pupils access to outdoor learning through outdoor activity clubs of schemes such as the Duke of Edinburgh Award Scheme.

Participation in outdoor activities can lead to learning opportunities in other curriculum areas. For example, geography or science-based work can involve significant physical activity as part of searches or navigation.

Overcoming barriers to outdoor learning

A mindset that is totally focused on safety does pupils and young people no favours. Far from keeping them safe from harm, it can deny them the very experiences that help them to learn how to handle the challenges that life may throw at them (Gill 2010: 3). This view is shared by the DfES (2006) who state that it is also vital that pupils learn how to manage challenge and risk for themselves in everyday situations so that they become confident and capable adults.

The myths that abound about risks and dangers can be a significant barrier to participation in many outdoor activities. Gill (2010) identifies several where teachers should appreciate that the reality is very different from the impression often given by the media.

1   The number of school visits is in serious decline. Despite media claims to this effect and statements in Parliament implying that school trips are coming to an end, statistics suggest otherwise. For example, from 2003–4 to 2005–6, activity trips in Worcestershire high schools grew by 230 per cent from 240 to 640 trips notified to the local authority.
2   Visits and outdoor activities are excessively dangerous. The impression is sometimes given that pupils come to serious harm on a regular basis when on educational visits. The reality is that travelling to and from school poses a comparable level of risk to that involved in

engagement in outings and activities. As Gill states (2010: 10) 'on a typical school visit, children are at no greater risk of death than their classmates who have stayed behind'.

3   Teachers face a serious risk of prosecution. Related to this is a notion that litigation is approaching epidemic proportions. In fact teachers are rarely personally sued and, as noted by the Health and Safety Executive (HSE) Chair Judith Hackitt (Hackitt 2008), on the rare occasions when this has happened, the teachers concerned have ignored direct instructions. Furthermore, legal claims appear to be reducing rather than increasing in number according to Fulbrook (2005).

4   Teaching unions are advising teachers not to lead or take part in educational visits. Contrary to popular belief this is not the case. While the NAS/UWT advises teachers to think carefully before becoming involved, it has, nevertheless, given its support to the Learning Outside the Classroom Manifesto. In response to a DCSF consultation in 2010 the union noted that learning outside the classroom could provide valuable educational experience and curriculum enrichment provided it is planned, properly resourced, linked to the curriculum and has clearly identified intended learning outcomes.

Guidance for teachers is available from a number of sources. Local authorities provide guidance for teachers that covers risk management or risk–benefit assessment. The latter approach involves looking at both the risks and the benefits of an activity and making a judgement based on both. It recognizes the importance of managing rather than eliminating risk and is being adopted by bodies including the HSE and the Department for Education.

The HSE (2000) itself publishes guidance on school trips, at the same time endorsing the educational value of well planned visits and supporting outdoor education. A key source of guidance is that provided by the Department for Education (DfES 1998).

In the specific context of physical education the Association for Physical Education offers safety guidelines for a wide range of activities undertaken in schools, including OAA (Whitlam and Beaumont 2008).

Summary

This chapter has introduced the reader to the potential of the outdoors as a learning environment. Its richness lies in its ability to promote activity, learning of physical skills in a different context, personal challenge and development together with core skills such as communication and teamwork and learning related to a whole range of curriculum subjects or areas of experience. The outdoors has special qualities that make it challenging and it is much less predictable than a classroom. Some activities can only take place outside but there are others that could be done inside but are enhanced by an outdoor context (Waite and Rea 2007).

To sum up:

- Outdoor learning can take place in a range of locations, including school grounds and residential settings.
- Much outdoor learning can be developed without the need for specialist training or equipment.
- Perceived barriers to outdoor education and learning are often based on inaccurate information.
- The benefits of outdoor learning range from those specific to physical education, to learning in other subject areas and to key developmental areas such as personal, social and emotional development.

10 The teacher as researcher

Introduction

This chapter provides some contextual information about teachers as researchers and about the advantages of engaging in research, together with practical information to help the teacher who wishes to become involved in research. It is, arguably, important to note that the position of teacher as researcher remains contentious. The notion of teacher as researcher follows much criticism of educational research as insufficiently relevant to classroom teachers (Clipson-Boyes 2000), as failing to inform practice (Hargreaves 1996) or influence policy (Hillage, Pearson et al. 1998), as frequently of questionable quality (Pring 1995; Tooley and Darby 1998) and as lacking clarity of purpose (Ranson 1996). Although teachers as researchers were proposed as long ago as 1975 (Stenhouse 1975), and have been supported by higher education and others for decades, Campbell et al. (2004) suggest that the value of teachers undertaking research has yet to be fully appreciated. Moreover, while Hargreaves (1996) sees teacher involvement in research as part of the solution, others, such as Huberman (1996), are trenchant critics of teachers as researchers, casting doubt upon whether any such work by teachers is entitled to be described as research. It is, then, hardly surprising that many teachers see research as something rather daunting, not something that they would be engaged with and perhaps done by others to them.

A variety of recent initiatives has attempted to involve teachers more centrally as researchers in their own schools. It would, however, be a mistake to see the current focus on teacher research as new. Throughout the 1970s and 1980s, teachers were funded, often through secondments, to take university-based courses that included significant research elements.

Support for teachers as researchers has been growing for some time through a variety of avenues. A significant shift towards school-based professional development has led to more teachers becoming involved in the planning and completion of small-scale projects. The introduction of Masters level credit to most PGCE courses has created opportunities for trainee teachers to engage in research. Much of this work is based upon action research although the term 'practitioner research' has become more widely used to denote an approach that is rather more inclusive and eclectic. It also avoids some of the problems that arise from the differences in nature and process advocated by different action research proponents. Moreover, the recently launched Masters in Teaching and Learning (MTL) (TDA 2010b) uses small-scale, work-based investigations as an important element of teachers' ongoing development. These developments are set against a move towards a greater use of evidence-based practice and increased engagement of teachers supported by various agencies including the TDA, National College for School Leadership (NCSL) and the National Teacher Research Panel (NTRP). In the wider social context, teacher engagement with research mirrors a broader trend towards the involvement of large numbers of professionals in research as part of professional development. This is in comparison with an earlier tendency for research to be associated with a small elite of professionals and full-time researchers (Denscombe 2003).

What is research?

The boundary between reflective practice and research is not clear and there are various contradictory views about where it should be drawn. Campbell et al. (2004) see reflective practitioners as, by definition, researchers, in that they not only research their own professional context but research that context from the inside – that is, as they act within it. They go on to suggest that this research may be tacit in that teachers adjust their behaviour to accommodate the complex situations within which they are acting. Taylor (2006) also suggests that practitioners in education engage in research within the day-to-day routines of work in school.

Personal engagement in research such as action research on a modest scale offers opportunities for individual teachers or small groups of colleagues to continue to develop their practice based upon critical and informed analysis of their working context. The British Educational Research Association (BERA) makes the distinction between policy/practice-focused research concerned with practical wisdom and discipline-focused research concerned with advancing theoretical knowledge (BERA 2010). The former has clear relevance to the primary school teacher. Bassey (1999: 38) defines research as 'systematic, critical and self-critical enquiry which aims to contribute to the advancement of knowledge and wisdom' and action researchers as 'teachers or managers who are trying to make beneficial change within their own workplace . . . Action researchers are using systematic and critical enquiry in attempts to improve their practical situation' (Bassey 1999: 41). It is this concern with improvements to practice that makes research of such significance to the primary school teacher who wishes to reflect on and develop their own teaching.

The sorts of research that teachers tend to engage in include those described as action research or practitioner research. While there are those who have sought to distinguish between the two, there is no real consensus about the differences or, indeed, whether there is any real difference. Dadds (1998) defines practitioner research as forms of enquiry that people undertake in their own working contexts and, usually, on their professional work in whatever sphere they practise. This definition would apply equally to action research although different writers would add a variety of other conditions that would have to be met for a project to be described as action research. For the purpose of this chapter, the terms will be treated as interchangeable.

We can see from this that all teachers have the capacity to be researchers – that is, to become involved in the systematic investigation of their own or others' practice. There are undoubtedly benefits to undertaking this kind of work with others. The motivation to complete work is likely to be enhanced by working with others. The impact of the work is likely to be wider and the data or information upon which decisions about future practice are made will probably be richer. That said, there is much to be gained from the individual teacher researching practice with his or her own class and using the results of information that has been collected and analysed systematically in order to improve practice.

Why get involved?

There has been considerable recent support for teachers as researchers from a variety of sources. The TLRP (2009) emphasized the importance of teachers having opportunities to undertake reflective, collaborative, classroom-focused enquiry in order to develop a well informed approach to their own learning and career.

A recent NTRP paper suggests that research carried out by teachers can have the following benefits:

- enabling teachers to learn to plan and teach more effectively;
- helping to develop informed professional judgement;
- enhancing teachers' skills, knowledge and understanding;
- encouraging collaborative working between teachers;
- improving pupils' learning and achievement;
- being manageable and highly cost effective; and
- enhancing teacher self-esteem and commitment to the profession and their job (NTRP 2003).

The NCSL uses the concept of the research-engaged school, described as follows, to highlight the advantages of teachers engaging in school-based research:

> In the research-engaged school, research and enquiry are integral to learning and teaching. They are built into the school's culture, outlook, systems and activity. Self-evaluation is not undertaken to satisfy some external demand but is integral to the day-to-day practice of the school and the classroom.
>
> Teachers in the research-engaged school:
>
> - have a desire for evidence and are inquisitive about learning and teaching
> - recognize that existing research may already provide useful intelligence about practice but are critical of received wisdom
> - have confidence in the research process
> - enjoy mutual support in exploring their thinking and scrutinizing their practice.
>
> Groups within and beyond the school collaborate on research and enquiry activity. They find ways of supporting research and enquiry; making it more rigorous, transparent and of value not only to the school itself but to a wider constituency.
>
> (NCSL 2009)

Sachs (1999) gives four reasons for engaging in research as a teacher:

- as a strategy for a broader change initiative within a school or classroom;
- for the improvement of classroom practice;
- as a contribution to an understanding of the teachers' knowledge base;
- as a basis for teacher professional development.

More specific to physical education, the Outdoor Learning Manifesto gives support to the use of action research by all involved with pupils and young people in order to explore different approaches (DfES 2006). The Association of Physical Education's National College for Professional Development uses an action research approach to develop teachers' capabilities.

Arguably, the single most important reason for teachers to become researchers, albeit on a small scale, is that it gives them the evidence and the power to evaluate, change and improve their practice. It has the potential to give individual primary teachers the knowledge and the confidence to be able to say to colleagues, parents, governors and other interested parties that they have investigated matters themselves and are basing their practice or changes in practice on evidence that they have found in relation to their pupils.

Action-based or practitioner research

Elliott (1991) describes the purpose of action research as the improvement of practice rather than the production of knowledge, a purpose that Sachs (1999) also ascribes to action or practitioner research. That is, rather than seeking knowledge that may or may not be used subsequently to influence practice, the primary aim of action or practitioner research is to bring about change in order to improve some element of practice. Bassey (1998) is consistent with this in defining action research as enquiry carried out to understand, evaluate and change in order to improve practice. Likewise, Cohen and Manion (1994) see action research as a procedure designed to deal with a concrete problem in a specific and immediate situation. All three capture the significant feature of action research, which is that it is about the influencing of practice by the researcher, who, in the context of this book, will be the teacher.

Reflective activity

Last year, Darren taught his Year Four class games using a range of teaching styles. These included reciprocal teaching during a unit of work on racket games, a games-making unit where problem solving was central and an invasion games unit in which he used more direct teaching but with a great deal of questioning. He feels that the pupils gain different things from the different approaches but he is not sure which are most effective. Now he wants to increase his understanding of the range of learning outcomes that each approach achieves. He decides to split each unit into two parts and to use a different main teaching style for each. He begins by teaching the first part of the racket games unit using more direct teaching and the second part using a reciprocal style where pupils work in 3s, with two players and one observer. After each lesson the pupils are asked to complete a chart that invites them to assess specific aspects of their learning on a five-point scale, including improved skill, improved ability to analyse their play, the ability to help someone else improve, and knowledge about the game. He uses the results from this phase of the project to plan his teaching approaches for his invasion games unit in order to attempt to broaden the range of the pupils' achievement.

- How does Darren's approach fit with your understanding of action research?

The most important factor for the teacher involved in research is that it should be fit for purpose – that is, it serves the need that it has been planned to meet.

In one of few published pieces to focus upon action research in the physical education context, Kirk (1995) identifies six key features that he claims are characteristic of action research that can contribute to the improvement of practice:

- Action research is collaborative in that, although it is possible for individuals to investigate their own practice on their own, it is likely that there will be greater benefits in terms of effectiveness, understanding and change when people who share a common interest or who are each affected by a physical education or sport programme participate together in action research.

Example

Downside Primary School identified the playground as an under-used resource. The Key Stage 1 team worked together to investigate the problem. They observed the pupils in the playground and compared their observations. Each teacher talked with their class about what the pupils did at playtime and why. The outcome was a range of issues that would not have surfaced had a single member of staff worked with their own class only.

- Action research is participatory and self-managed, that is, the research agenda is controlled by the people whose practices are the topic of enquiry so that it provides outcomes that are meaningful and beneficial to all participants.
- Action research is data-based – that is, it is not simply what teachers normally do when they teach but it involves the systematic collection of information on which to base reflection and action.

Example

Downside's Key Stage 1 team drew up a recording sheet so that their playground observations had some consistency. This included levels of activity, whether pupils were active on their own or in groups, the composition of the groups (boys/girls, same class/age, mix of class/age), choice of activity and the use made of the resources available in the playground. Their analysis of these observations formed the basis of key questions used in conversations with the pupils. These were recorded as field notes.

- Action research involves reflection – that is, an active process of engaging intellectually with information about the topic under investigation.
- Action research is situated – that is, it involves looking in on practice and, at the same time, looking out to see whether those practices are located alongside or within other, broader social and educational practices.
- Action research is reform-oriented – that is, it is justified on the basis of its practical consequences, rather than being research for the sake of doing research.

Example

The outcomes of Downside's project included zoning the playground with discrete activity areas; separate 'quiet areas' for those who wanted to sit and talk; the provision of more small games and play equipment for the pupils' use; and training for teaching assistants and supervisors in encouraging and monitoring the use of the space and the equipment. The project thus led to a number of practical changes that will be monitored in the future.

Most action research is based on a cyclical model (see Figure 10.1). The research feeds directly into practice by identifying issues and instigating change, so it is also ongoing in that the impact of the change then needs to be researched, further change introduced as necessary and the whole process starts again. In the context of the primary school, the teacher's starting point is likely to be an issue in relation to some aspect of current practice. In order to identify potential solutions or changes, information or data need to be gathered to understand better the nature of the issue. Once this information has been collected it can be analysed and conclusions drawn. On the basis of the evidence collected and its analysis, changes can be proposed and implemented, at which point the cycle may start again. The whole process can thus be ongoing, although, for practical purposes, teachers are likely to work on a single cycle, especially if they are planning to disseminate their findings to colleagues or a wider audience, or submit them as part of an award-bearing professional development programme such as a postgraduate certificate or Masters qualification.

This model or variations of it forms the basis of much current professional development work including the National PE and School Sport Development Programme and much Masters Level assessed work.

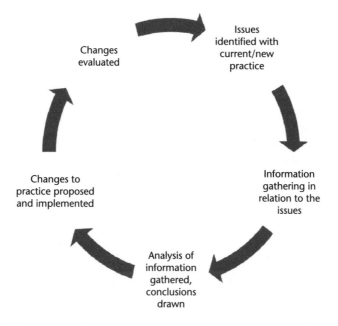

Figure 10.1   Action research-based cycle.

Ethics and teacher researchers

Doyle (2003), writing for the NTRP, notes that 'With so many teachers researching, questions of ethics and ethical guidelines will arise including the importance and rights of the individuals involved. These individuals will include the researcher, colleagues and parents. Pupils will inevitably be participants in the research.'

Student teachers or those undertaking research projects as part of higher education programmes will almost certainly be governed by the ethical guidelines of the institution with which they are registered. Teachers working independently of other organizations will need to consider the ethical issues involved in their work.

The fact that pupils are highly likely to be a part of the research process raises some important issues that have not always been given sufficient attention. Lindsay (2000) notes that the BERA ethical guidance, along with that of other codes of conduct, makes little explicit reference to issues related to research involving pupils, although revised BERA (2004) guidelines do address the issue of pupils and research. Anderson (2004) notes that while education research, unlike some medical research, is unlikely to kill or maim, it can nevertheless upset, worry, embarrass or betray.

Key ethical principles are identified by BERA (2004) as follows:

- Voluntary informed consent – ensuring that participants understand the process in which they are to be involved and give their consent prior to its start. Where pupils are too young to give consent then this must be obtained from an appropriate adult.
- Avoidance of deception – an element of ensuring that informed consent has been obtained.
- Right to withdraw – ensuring that participants are aware that they may withdraw their consent at any time.
- Consideration of the best interests of the child – this includes the need to facilitate pupils to give fully informed consent in accordance with Article 12 of the United Nations Convention on the Rights of the Child.
- Incentives – these should be 'commensurate with good sense'.
- Privacy – the need to recognize participants' right to privacy and to work within data protection legislation.

These issues should be considered carefully by the primary school teacher. In practice, teachers are likely to be guided by policy within their own school. This should clarify matters such as consent and give advice about when consent can be given by the head teacher and when it should be sought from parents or individual pupils. It is particularly important when an action research approach is being used because the boundaries between individual reflective research and that which involves the participation of others, including pupils, are not always clear.

Doyle (2003) makes an important ethical point when he notes that, although research might be part of the teacher's professional development, the pupils are not there for the teacher's development. The opposite is the case in that the teacher is there for the development of the pupils. He points out that, while the two are linked in that it is in the interest of the child that the teacher is a better teacher, the child's participation should not be taken for granted. This is not to discourage teachers from researching but is to draw attention to the importance of considering how to ensure that due attention is paid to ethical issues related to the pupils involved.

Reflective activity

Jane is finding it difficult to keep her whole class engaged in dance lessons. Keeping the interest of both boys and girls is especially challenging. She decides to get the class to write about their dance experiences over a period of a term and then to discuss their writing in small groups. Her plan is to present her findings to the rest of the staff and then, possibly, to a meeting of the local primary school cluster.

- Is Jane engaged in research or is she simply using a cross-curricular approach to improve pupil engagement and achievement?
- At what point does her work become research?
- How might she ensure that the ethical principles of informed consent and confidentiality are upheld?

Project planning

Here is one example of a teacher research project that stems from a wish to address a growing problem with Years Five and Six where pupils seem to be less motivated in physical education than previously. James, as physical education manager, wants to understand what is happening and develop some strategies to improve the situation.

Developing research questions

Having identified patchy interest in physical education at Southwick Junior School, with some children seeming to lose interest altogether and others diffi-cult to engage in some activity areas, the next stage is to develop questions that will help to narrow the focus and ensure that the project is manageable and has the potential to lead to some practical ways forward. It is important to ensure that what is attempted is suitable in scale and can be completed in a reasonable and realistic timescale (see Table 10.1).

Choosing research approaches and techniques

Evidence is needed in order to answer the research question. Evidence comes in a range of forms, including interviews/discussions (with individuals or groups), pupils' work, observations, questionnaires, documentation such as policies, notes of meetings, personal journals or field notes, video recordings, photographs or audio tapes. In order to decide what kind of evidence is needed, and potential sources, it will be helpful to break the initial question down into sub-questions:

- How do different pupils feel about their current physical education experience?
- What do staff think are the issues when teaching physical education to Years Five and Six pupils?

Table 10.1 Suitability of research questions

Draft research question	Goldilocks test	Russian doll principle
1 What's going wrong with Key Stage 2 physical education at Southwick School?	Too big	This question requires several smaller questions before the study could be designed round it.
2 Which teachers can successfully motivate Key Stage 2 pupils in physical education at Southwick School?	Too hot	Naming successful teachers is not a desirable outcome. But the attitudes and practices of the successful teachers might be useful.
3 What prevents motivation in physical education at Southwick and how can it be improved?	Just right	Perhaps should be more clearly addressed. Questions need refining further.
4 How can we improve motivation for Key Stage 2 physical education at Southwick School?	Just right	This question should help to identify current practice and possible solutions followed by some trialling and evaluation of some new practices.

(after Clough and Nutbrown 2002)

- How do pupils respond to different activities and tasks in physical education lessons?

James decides to interview Years Five and Six pupils in groups. As one of the issues is the behaviour of some boys in dance lessons, he decides to interview single-sex groups. He also decides to ask the head for a staff meeting discussion about the issue and plans to tape record this for later analysis. He also asks two colleagues to record two examples of physical education lessons.

Ethical issues

The decisions made above raise a number of ethical issues. James already has the support of his head teacher. He also needs the informed consent of the pupils he is to interview so he prepares an information sheet that includes key information and a summary of the project and asks the class to complete this with a countersignature from their parents. A similar information sheet is written for the staff who are invited to take part in the discussion, which is arranged as the final staff meeting item so that any who do not wish to take part can leave.

In order to video a lesson, pupil and parental consent is also needed. Two parents do not give consent so the teachers involved are careful to ensure that these pupils are never in camera shot. The pupils work in the same group to facilitate this.

Collecting information/data

James decides to collect his information over a four-week timespan. This gives him time to interview pupil groups during lunch breaks where he does not have other commitments and for the teachers to organize and record lessons. Twenty Year Five and 18 Year Six pupils provide parental consent by James's deadline. As each group has a good mix of boys and girls and pupils of varying ability levels James decides to work with these pupils rather than following up those who have not returned consent forms. The interviews are conducted with groups of four or five boys or girls, four groups from each class. Each group interview lasts for approximately 40 minutes. A staff meeting in the third week of his data collection period includes his project as an agenda item. All staff take part.

Analysing information collected

James identifies the main themes emerging from the group interviews first. He then uses the minutes of the staff meeting and the recorded lessons to triangulate his findings and to check for any important additional themes that did not appear in the interview material. His initial findings are that:

- Falling levels of interest appear to stem from a mix of activity-specific reasons and contextual issues.
- Both boys and girls dislike playing games in mixed-gender groups. The more able point out that they play in single-gender teams outside school and prefer this. Some less able girls feel that being made to work in groups with boys adds to their embarrassment at their own limitations. Staff comment on silly behaviour from some groups and on the difficulty of motivating a small group of less able girls. They suggest that some of these pupils would benefit from using modified equipment.
- Both boys and girls dislike the topics used as the basis for dance lessons. The boys think that they are 'sissy' and the girls think that they are boring and encourage the boys to misbehave. Some of the girls have friends at a school that linked dance with their history topic and want to know why they cannot do something similar. Staff identify boys' behaviour in dance as the major physical education issue.

- Boys and girls are both unhappy with changing arrangements that give them no privacy. A small minority deliberately forget their physical education kit because of this.

Drawing conclusions

James's project is small-scale, involving two classes in one school. His conclusions are, therefore, likely to be specific to his school although they may well apply to other schools. In writing his report, he expresses his conclusions to make it clear that they are not necessarily generalizable and that, as in most educational research, they are fairly tentative at this stage. His initial conclusions are that:

- Negotiating group/team membership and allowing single-gender groups and teams may improve motivation in games.
- A choice of equipment (especially balls and rackets) may help less able pupils to achieve.
- Using dance topics that link to other curriculum areas or that have been suggested by the pupils may improve motivation and behaviour.
- There should be further discussion on how to improve changing arrangements. He proposes using the hall and the classroom to create two spaces (Years Five and Six have classrooms almost adjacent to the hall).

Writing up

James writes a short report for his head teacher and prepares a PowerPoint presentation for the staff that he subsequently uses with local initial teacher training (ITT) students. He writes a longer report and this is submitted together with the PowerPoint presentation as the assessed work for one project module in his Masters programme.

Disseminating

Arguably, what distinguishes small-scale research from reflective practice is the process of sharing and disseminating the outcomes. This may take the form of submission for assessment towards, for example, a Postgraduate Certificate or a Masters degree. It could involve presenting findings at a staff meeting for discussion, or to other physical education managers in a primary cluster. Some CPD programmes publish collections of the projects completed by teachers as part of their course or place them on the web where they can be shared with the wider education community. Publication of research in the form of reports, articles or conference papers is the norm within higher education. Sachs (1999) makes the point that action research, where the aim is the improvement of practice, may well be disseminated less formally and through relatively ephemeral types of communication represented in talk and dialogue. She also stresses that the 'least inclusive level of documenting and reporting – in this case the local public domain of the particular school as a learning community – is no less important than the more inclusive levels' (Sachs 1999: 50). In this case, James shares his findings and analysis with the staff in his school and they discuss the implications for changes in practice that he has identified. He is subsequently invited to talk about his project with primary initial teacher training students at his local university.

Because this is an action research-based project, it does not end here. The changes that James has proposed based on his findings form the start of a further cycle in which the impact of the changes would be assessed, analysed and discussed.

Summary

This chapter has shown how all teachers have the potential to engage in research and has demonstrated that research is a legitimate and rewarding activity for the teacher.

To summarize:

- Research serves different purposes, some of which require large-scale data collection and analysis and some of which may be undertaken by an individual in their own working context.
- All teachers have the capacity to be engaged in research.
- Although much can be achieved by teachers researching their own practice, working with others can add richness to the outcomes, broaden the potential relevance of the research and help with motivation to complete.
- Engagement with research has the potential to further professional development, improve practice and raise achievement.
- Sharing the outcomes of research through dissemination within the school or more widely is a key part of the process.

Glossary

BERA	British Educational Research Association
DCMS	Department for Culture Media and Sport
DCSF	Department for Children Schools and Families
DfEE	Department for Education and Employment
DfES	Department for Education and Science
EAL	English as an Additional Language
EOC	Equal Opportunities Commission
EYFS	Early Years Foundation Stage
GCSE	General Certificate of Secondary Education
HSE	Health and Safety Executive
ITT	Initial teacher training
MTL	Masters in Teaching and Learning
NACCCE	National Advisory Committee on Creative and Cultural Education
NCSL	National College for School Leadership
NTRP	National Teacher Research Project
OAA	Outdoor and Adventurous Activities
OfSTED	Office for Standards in Education
PESS	Physical Education and School Sport
PESSCL	Physical Education and School Sport and Club Links
PESSYP	Physical Education and Sport Strategy for Young People
QCA	Qualifications and Curriculum Authority
QCDA	Qualifications and Curriculum Development Agency
SEAL	Social and Emotional Aspects of Learning
TDA	Training and Development Agency for Schools
TLRP	Teaching and Learning Research Project

Bibliography

Alexander, K. and Penney, D. (2005) Teaching under the influence: feeding Games for Understanding into the Sport Education development-refinement cycle, *Physical Education and Sport Pedagogy*, 10(3): 287–301.

Alexander, R. (2009) *Towards a New Primary Curriculum: A Report from the Cambridge Primary Review. Part 2: The Future*. Cambridge: University of Cambridge Faculty of Education.

Anderson, G.J. with Arsenault, N. (2004) *Fundamentals of Educational Research*. 2nd edn. London: RoutledgeFalmer.

Andrews, C. (2005) *Meeting SEN in the Curriculum: PE/Sports*. London: David Fulton Publishers.

Arnold, P.J. (1979) *Meaning in Movement, Sport and Physical Education*. London: Heinemann.

Assessment Reform Group (2002) *Assessment for Learning – Ten Principles: Research-Based Principles to Guide Classroom Practice*. Assessment Reform Group. London: ARG.

BAALPE, PEAUK, PEITT Network (2005) *Declaration from the National Summit on Physical Education*. London: CCPR.

Bailey, R. and Macfadyen, T. (eds) (2000) *Teaching Physical Education, 5–11*. London: Continuum.

Bassey, M. (1998) Action research for improving practice, in R. Halsall (ed.), *Teacher Research and School Improvement: Opening Doors from the Inside*. Buckingham: Open University Press.

Bassey, M. (1999) *Case Study Research in Educational Settings*. Buckingham: Open University Press.

Bell, J. (2005) *Doing your Research Project*. 4th edn. Maidenhead: Open University Press.

BERA (2004) *Revised Ethical Guidelines for Educational Research*. Macclesfield: BERA.

BERA (2010) *Who we are*, www.bera.ac.uk/about-2/who-we-are (accessed 13 November 2010).

Black, P. and Wiliam, D. (1998a) Assessment and Classroom Learning, *Assessment in Education*, 5(1): 7–75.

Black, P. and Wiliam, D. (1998b) *Inside the Black Box: Raising Standards through Classroom Assessment*. London: School of Education, King's College.

Bloom, B.S. (1956) *Taxonomy of Educational Objectives: The Cognitive Dimension*. New York: McKay.

Boden, M.A. (1990) *The Creative Mind: Myths and Mechanisms*. London: Weidenfeld & Nicolson.

Browne, A. (2004) Special Educational Needs in Mainstream Primary Schools, in A. Browne and D. Haylock (eds) *Professional Issues for Primary Teachers*. London: Paul Chapman Publishing.

Campbell, A., McNamara, O. and Gilroy, P. (2004) *Practitioner Research and Professional Development in Education*. London: Paul Chapman Publishing.

Capel, S. (2005) Teachers, teaching and pedagogy in physical education, in K. Green and K. Hardman (eds) *Physical Education, Essential Issues*. London: Sage.

Carroll, B. (1994) *Assessment in Physical Education: A Teacher's Guide to the Issues*. London: The Falmer Press.

Carter, A. (1998) *The Routledge Dance Studies Reader*. London: Routledge.

Carter, K. and Halsall, R. (1998) Teacher research for school improvement, in R. Halsall (ed.) *Teacher Research and School Improvement: Opening Doors from the Inside*. Buckingham: Open University Press.

Casbon, C. and Spackman, L. (2005) *Assessment for Learning in Physical Education*. Worcester: BAALPE.

CfSA (2008) Physical education, supporting gifted and talented children, *Primary Matters 2*, Autumn.

CfSA (2009) *Physical Education, Learning Outside the Classroom*. London: CfSA.

Chappell, R. (1995) Racial stereotyping in schools, *Bulletin of PE*, 31(4): 22–8.

Cliffe, J.E. (2008) Emotional intelligence and school leadership: testing for and evaluating the role of emotional intelligence in a group of female secondary school leaders. Unpublished PhD thesis, Manchester Metropolitan University.

Cliffe, J.E. (in press) Emotional intelligence: a study of secondary female headteachers, *Educational Management Administration and Leadership*.

Clipson-Boyes, S. (2000) *Putting Research into Practice in Primary Teaching and Learning*. London: David Fulton.

Clough, P. and Nutbrown, G. (2002) *A Student's Guide to Methodology*. London: Sage.

Cohen, L. and Manion, L. (1994) *Research Methods in Education*. London: Routledge.

Connolly, P. (2003) *Boys and Schooling in the Early Years*. London: RoutledgeFalmer.

Cooper, G. (1998) *Outdoors with Young People*. Lyme Regis: Russell House Publishing.

Craft, A. (2006) Fostering creativity with wisdom, *Cambridge Journal of Education*, 36(3): 337–50.

Cropley, A.J. (2001) *Creativity in Education and Learning: A Guide for Teachers and Educators*. London: Kogan Page.

Curtner-Smith, M., McCaughtry, N. and Lacon, S. (2001) Urban teachers' use of productive and reproductive teaching styles within the confines of the national curriculum for physical education, *European Physical Education Review*, 7(2): 177–90.

Dadds, M. (1998) Supporting practitioner research: a challenge, *Educational Action Research*, 6(1): 39–52.

DCSF (2007) *The Children's Plan: Building Brighter Futures*. London: HMSO.

DCSF (2008a) *Statutory Framework for the Early Years Foundation Stage*. Nottingham: DCSF.

DCSF (2008b) *The Bercow Report: A Review of Services for Children and Young People (0–19) with Speech, Language and Communication Needs*. Nottingham: DCSF.

DCSF (2008c) *The Assessment for Learning Strategy*. Nottingham: DCSF.

DCSF (2009) *Inclusion*. www.nationalstrategies.standards.dcsf.gov.uk/inclusion (accessed 13 November 2010).

DCSF (2010) *Practical Strategies to Support the Whole-School Development of AFL work with APP (Primary)*. Nottingham: DCSF.

Denscombe, M. (2003) *The Good Research Guide*. 2nd edn. Maidenhead: Open University Press.

DfEE (1997) *Excellence in Schools*. London: HMSO.

DfEE/QCA (1999) *Physical Education – the National Curriculum for England*. London: QCA.

DfES (1998) *Health and Safety of Pupils on Educational Visits*. London: DfES.

DfES (2003a) *Every Child Matters*. London: DfES.

DfES (2003b) *Excellence and Enjoyment: A Strategy for Primary Schools*. London: DfES.

DfES (2004) *High Quality PE and Sport for Young People*. London: DfES.

DfES (2005) *Do You Have High Quality PE and Sport in Your School? A Guide to Self-evaluating and Improving the Quality of PE and School Sport*. Annesley: DfES.

DfES (2006) *Learning Outside the Classroom: Manifesto*. Nottingham: DfES.

DfES and DCMS (2003) *Learning through PE and Sport*. London: DfES.

Dismore, H. and Bailey, R. (2005) If only: outdoor and adventurous activities and generalised academic development, *Journal of Adventure Education and Outdoor Learning*, 5: 9–19.

Doherty, J. and Bailey, R. (2003) *Supporting Physical Development and Physical Education in the Early Years*. Buckingham: Open University Press.

Doyle, D. (2003) *Transdisciplinary Enquiry – Researching With rather than Researching On*. www.standards.dfes.gov.uk/ourwork/hostingresearch/(accessed 3 October 2009).

Elliott, J. (1991) *Action Research for Educational Change*. Milton Keynes: Open University Press.

Epstein, D. (ed.) (1998) *Failing Boys? Issues in Gender and Achievement*. Buckingham: Open University Press.

Fisher, R. and Williams, M. (eds) (2004) *Unlocking Creativity: A Teacher's Guide to Creativity Across the Curriculum*. London: David Fulton.

Frapwell, A. (2009) Narrative matters: physical education and learning outside the classroom, *Primary PE Matters*, 4: vi–vii.

Fulbrook, J. (2005) *Outdoor Activities, Negligence and the Law*. Aldershot: Ashgate Publishing.

Gallahue, D.L. (1976) *Motor Development and Movement Experiences for Young Children*. New York: John Wiley & Sons.

Gallahue, D.L. and Ozmun, J.C. (1998) *Understanding Motor Development and Movement Experiences: Infants, Children, Adolescents, Adults*. 4th edn. Boston, MA: McGraw-Hill.

Gardner, H. (1999) *Intelligence Reframed*. New York: Basic Books.

Gill, T. (2010) *Nothing Ventured . . . Balancing Risks and Benefits in the Outdoors*. London: English Outdoor Council.

Goleman, D. (1995) *Emotional Intelligence: Why It Can Matter More than IQ*. London: Bloomsbury.

Green, K. and Hardman, K. (eds) (2005) *Physical Education, Essential Issues*. London: Sage.

GTCE (2006) *Using Research in Your School and Your Teaching – Research Engaged Professional Practice*. www.gtce.org.uk/documents/publicationspdfs/tplf_research_tp060106.pdf (accessed 3 October 2009).

Hardy, C. and Mawer, M. (eds) (1999) *Learning and Teaching in Physical Education*. London: Falmer Press.

Hargreaves, D. (1996) *Teaching as a Research-Based Profession*. TTA Annual Lecture 1996, originally retrieved from www.tda.gov.uk.

Harris, J. and Cale, L. (1997) Activity promotion in physical education, *European Physical Education Review*, 3(1): 58–67.

Hayes, D. (ed.) (2007) *Joyful Teaching and Learning in the Primary School*. Exeter: Learning Matters.

Hayes, S. and Stidder, G. (eds) (2003) *Equity and Inclusion in Physical Education and Sport*. London: Routledge.

Health and Safety Executive (HSE) (2000) *School Trips*. www.hse.gov.uk/school-trips/index.htm (accessed 13 November 2010).

Hillage, J., Pearson, R., Anderson, A. and Tamkin, P. (1998) *Excellence in Research on Schools, Research Report No. 74*. London: DfEE.

House of Commons (2005) *Education Outside the Classroom: Select Committee on Education and Skills Second Report*. London: HMSO.

Huberman, M. (1996) Focus on research moving mainstream: taking a closer look at teacher research, *Language Arts*, 73: 124–40.

Hughes, M. (2002) *Tweak to Transform*. Stafford: Network Educational Press.

Humberstone, B. (1992) Outdoor Education in the National Curriculum, in N. Armstrong (ed.) *New Directions in Physical Education, Volume 2, Towards a National Curriculum*. Leeds: Human Kinetics Books.

Kellam, R. and Whelwell, E. (2009) Linked learning and its place in the teaching of PE in the primary school, *Physical Education Matters*, 4(2): 24–8.

Kirk, D. (1988) *Physical Education and Curriculum Study*. London: Croom Helm.

Kirk, D. (1995) Action research and educational reform in physical education, *Pedagogy in Practice*, 1(1): 4–21.

Kirk, D. (2005) Physical education, youth sport and lifelong participation: the importance of early learning experiences, *European Physical Education Review*, 11(3): 239–55.

Kirk, D., Nauright, J., Harahan, D. and Jobling, I. (1996) *The Sociocultural Foundations of Human Movement*. South Melbourne: Macmillan Education Australia Ltd.

Knight, S. (2009) *Forest Schools and Outdoor Learning in the Early Years*. London: Sage.

Koshy, V. (2005) *Action Research for Improving Practice*. London: Paul Chapman Publishing.

Lewis, A. and Lindsay, G. (eds) (2000) *Researching Children's Perspectives*. Buckingham: Open University Press.

Lewis, V. (2004) Doing research with children and young people, in S. Fraser, V. Lewis, S. Ding, M. Kellett and C. Robinson (eds) *Doing Research with Children and Young People*. London: Sage with Open University Press.

Lindsay, G. (2000) Researching children's perspectives: ethical issues, in A. Lewis and G. Lindsay (eds) *Researching Children's Perspectives*. Buckingham: Open University Press.

LOTC (2008) *Case Study – LOTC Awards, National Winner Castlechurch Primary School*. London: DCSF.

Mawer, M. (1999) Teaching styles and teaching approaches in physical education research developments, in C. Hardy and M. Mawer (eds) *Learning and Teaching in Physical Education*. London: Falmer.

Middlewood, D., Coleman, M. and Lumby, J. (1999) *Practitioner Research in Education*. London: Paul Chapman Publishing.

Miles, H., Benn, T., Dagkas, S. and Jawad, H. (2008) Muslim Girls, physical education and school sport, *Physical Education Matters*, 3(4): 10–11.

Morgan, K. and Sproule, J. (2005) Effects of different teaching styles on the teacher behaviours that influence motivational climate and pupils' motivation in physical education, *European Physical Education Review*, 11(3): 257–85.

Morley, D. and Bailey, R. (2006) *Meeting the Needs of Your Most Able Pupils: Physical Education and Sport*. London: David Fulton.

Mosston, M. and Ashworth, S. (2002) *Teaching Physical Education: from Command to Discovery*. 5th edn. San Francisco: Cummings.

National Advisory Committee on Creative and Cultural Education (NACCCE) (1999) *All Our Futures*. London: DfEE and DCFS.

National Association for Advisors for Computers in Education (2007) *Primary Review: NAACE Position Paper*. www.naace.co.uk/217 (accessed 13 November 2010).

NCSL (2009) www.ncsl.org.uk/research_and_development/research_activities/randd-activities-engaged.cfm (accessed 20 September 2009).

Norfolk County Council (2010) *Outdoor and Adventurous Activities.* www.norfolk. gov.uk/myportal/index.cfm?s+1&m=1942&p=516,index (accessed 13 June 2010).

NTRP (2003) *National Teacher Research Panel's Guidelines for CPD Co-ordinators – Can Research Help?* www.standards.dfes.gov.uk/ntrp (accessed 3 October 2009).

Nundy, S., Dillon, J. and Dowd, P. (2009) Improving and encouraging teacher confidence in out-of-classroom learning: the impact of the Hampshire Trailblazer project on 3-13 curriculum practitioners, *Education, 3–13*, 37: 61–73.

OfSTED (2001) *Evaluating Educational Inclusion: Guidance for Inspectors and Schools.* London: HMSO.

OfSTED (2002) *The Curriculum in Successful Primary Schools.* London: OfSTED.

OfSTED (2003) *Expecting the Unexpected, Developing Creativity in Primary and Secondary Schools* e-publication, originally retrieved from www.ofsted.gov.uk.

OfSTED (2004) *Outdoor Education – Aspects of Good Practice.* London: OfSTED.

OfSTED (2005) *The Annual Report of Her Majesty's Inspector of Schools, 2004/5.* www. ofsted.gov.uk (accessed 22 September 2009).

OfSTED (2006) *The Importance of Cross Curricular Learning.* London: OfSTED.

OfSTED (2008a) *Learning Outside the Classroom: How Far Should You Go?* London: OfSTED.

OfSTED (2008b) *Assessment for Learning: The Impact of National Strategy Support.* London: OfSTED.

OfSTED (2009a) *Physical Education in Schools 2005–8, Working Towards 2012 and Beyond.* London: OfSTED.

OfSTED (2009b) *The Importance of ICT: Information and Communication Technology in Primary and Secondary Schools, 2005/2008.* London: OfSTED.

OfSTED (2010) *Learning: Creative Approaches that Raise Standards.* London: OfSTED.

OfSTED and EOC (1996) *The Gender Divide: Performance Differences Between Boys and Girls and School.* London: HMSO.

Outdoor Education Advisers Panel (2005) *High Quality Outdoor Education.* Lifton: English Outdoor Council.

Outward Bound Trust (2010) *First Challenge – A Case Study.* Durham: St Benet's RC Voluntary Aided Primary School.

Parsons, G. (2006) *Heading Out: Exploring the Impact of Outdoor Experiences on Young Children.* London: Learning Through Landscapes.

Penney, D. (ed.) (2002) *Gender and Physical Education, Contemporary Issues and Future Directions.* London: Routledge.

Penney, D. and Evans, J. (1999) *Politics Policy and Practice in Physical Education.* London: Spon.

PESS (2007) *Celebrating PESS: 2000–2007.* www.qcda.gov.uk/14405.aspx (accessed 15 January 2010).

PESSCL (2007a) *How are Schools using PESS to Improve Behaviour and Attitudes to Learning?* www.qcda.gov.uk/14405.aspx (accessed 15 January 2010).

PESSCL (2007b) *How are Schools using PESS to Raise Achievement across the Curriculum?* www.qcda.gov.uk/14405.aspx (accessed 15 January 2010).

Pickup, I. and Price, L. (2007) *Teaching Physical Education in the Primary School.* London: Continuum.

Piotrowski, S. (2000) Assessment, recording and reporting, in R. Bailey and T. Macfadyen (eds) *Teaching Physical Education 5–11.* London: Continuum.

Piotrowski, S. and Capel, S. (2000) Formal and informal modes of assessment in physical education, in S. Capel and S. Piotrowski (eds) *Issues in Physical Education.* London: Routledge Falmer.

Pring, R. (1995) Editorial, *British Journal of Educational Studies,* 42(2): 121–4.

Pritchard, A. (2005) *Ways of Learning, Learning Theories and Learning Styles in the Classroom.* London: David Fulton.

QCA (2005a) *Physical Education – 2004/5 Annual Report on Curriculum and Assessment.* London: QCA.

QCA (2005b) *Creativity: Find it Promote It! – Promoting Pupils' Creative Thinking and Behaviour Across the Curriculum at Key Stages 1, 2 and 3 – Practical Materials for Schools.* London: QCA.

QCA (2010) *Introducing the new Primary Curriculum, Guidance for Primary Schools.* Coventry: QCDA.

QCDA (1999) *National Curriculum Physical Education, Key Stages 1 and 2.* www.curriculum.qcda.gov.uk/key-stages-1-and-2/inclusion/statutory-inclusion-statement (accessed 11 December 2009).

QCDA (2000) *Outdoor and Adventurous Activities.* www.qcda.gov.uk (accessed 11 December 2009).

QCDA (2008) *Ours is a Shared Horizon, 2007 Annual Review.* www.qcda.gov.uk (accessed 22 September 2009).

QCDA (2010) *The National Curriculum Level Descriptions for subjects 2010.* Coventry: QCDA.

Quick, S., Dalziel, D., Thornton, A. and Simon, A. (2009) *PE and Sport Survey 2008/9, Research Report DCSF-RR168.* London: DCSF.

Radnor, H. (2002) *Researching Your Professional Practice.* Buckingham: Open University Press.

Rea, T. (2008) Alternative visions of learning: children's learning experiences in the outdoors, *Educational Futures,* 1(2): 42–50.

Ranson, S. (1996) The future of education research: learning at the centre, *British Educational Research Journal,* 22(5): 523–35.

Rink, J. (2002) *Teaching Physical Education for Learning.* New York: McGraw-Hill.

Robertson, E. (1994) *Physical Education, A Practical Guide, Key Stage 2.* London: John Murray.

Robinson, J.F. and Shallcross, T. (1998) Social change and education for sustainable living, *Pedagogy, Culture and Society,* 6(1): 69–84.

Rose, J. (2009) *Independent Review of the Primary Curriculum, Final Report.* London: DCSF.

Rosen, M. and Oxenbury, H. (1989) *We're Going on a Bear Hunt*. London: Walker Books Ltd.

Rowe, M.B. (1974) Wait time and rewards as instructional variables, their influence on language, logic and fate control, *Journal of Research in Science Teaching*, 11: 81–94.

Sachs, J. (1999) Using teacher research as a basis for professional renewal, *Professional Development in Education*, 25(1): 39–53.

Salovey, P. and Mayer, J.D. (1990) Emotional intelligence, *Imagination, Cognition and Personality*, 9: 185–211.

Sefton-Green, J. (2008) *Creative Learning*. London: The Arts Council.

Siedentop, D. and Tannehill, D. (2000) *Developing Teaching Skills in Physical Education*. Mountain View, CA: Mayfield.

Smith, J. (2004) Gender issues in primary schools, in A. Browne and D. Haylock (eds) *Professional Issues for Primary Teachers*. London: Paul Chapman.

Spackman, L. (2002) Assessment for learning: the lessons for physical education, *The Bulletin of Physical Education*, 38(3): 179–93.

Sparkes, A. (ed.) (1992) *Research in Physical Education and Sport, exploring alternative visions*. London: Falmer Press.

Sport England and Youth Sport Trust (2009) *The PE and Sport Strategy for Young People, A Guide to Delivering the Five Hour Offer*. London: Youth Sport Trust.

Steinberg, H., Sykes, E.A., Moss, T., et al. (1997) Exercise enhances creativity independently of mood, *British Journal of Sports Medicine*, May: 240–5.

Steiner, C. and Perry, P. (1997) *Achieving Emotional Literacy*. London: Bloomsbury.

Stenhouse, L. (1975) *An Introduction to Curriculum Research and Development*. London: Heinemann.

Taylor, C. (2006) Introducing action research, in C. Taylor, M. Wilkie and J. Baser (eds) *Doing Action Research, A Guide for School Support Staff*. London: Paul Chapman Publishing.

TDA (2010a) *Cross-Curricular Materials*. www.tda.gov.uk (accessed 15 July 2010).

TDA (2010b) *Masters in Teaching and Learning*. www.tda.gov.uk/teachers/mtl.aspx (accessed 13 November 2010).

Tinning, R. (1992) Action research as epistemology and practice: towards transformative educational practice in physical education, in A. Sparkes (ed.) *Research in Physical Education and Sport: Exploring Alternative Visions*. Brighton: Falmer Press.

TLRP (2009) *Impact and Significance, Teaching and Learning Research Programme*. www.tlrp.org.uk/pub/documents/ImpactLeaflet.pdf (accessed 7 October 2009).

Tooley, J. and Darby, D. (1998) *Educational Research: A Critique*. London: OfSTED.

Vickerman, P. and Coates, J. (2009) Trainee and recently qualified physical education teachers' perspectives on including children with special educational needs, *Physical Education and Sport Pedagogy*, 14(2): 137–53.

Vygotsky, L.S. (1978) *Mind in Society: The Development of Higher Psychological Processes*. Cambridge, MA: Harvard University Press.

Waite, S. and Rea, T. (2007) Enjoying teaching and learning outside the classroom, in D. Hayes (ed.) *Joyful Teaching and Learning in the Primary School*. Exeter: Learning Matters.

Whitehead, M. and Murdoch, E. (2006) Physical literacy and physical education, conceptual mapping, *PE Matters*, www.physical-literacy.org.uk/conceptual-mapping2006.php (accessed 23 March 2010).

Whitlam, P. and Beaumont, G. (2008) *Safe Practice in Physical Education and School Sport*. Leeds: Coachwise.

Williams, A. (1989) The place of physical education in primary education, in A. Williams (ed.) *Issues in Physical Education for the Primary Years*. London: Falmer Press.

Williams, A. (1996a) *Teaching Physical Education, A Guide for Mentors and Students*. London: David Fulton.

Williams, A. (1996b) Physical Education at Key Stage 2, in N. Armstrong (ed.) *New Directions in Physical Education*. London: Cassell.

Williams, A. (ed.) (2000) *Primary School Physical Education: Research into Practice*. London: Routledge Falmer.

Williams, E. A. and Bedward, J. (2000) An inclusive national curriculum? The experiences of adolescent girls, *European Journal of Physical Education*, 5(1): 4–18.

Woods, P. (1995) *Creative Teachers in Primary Schools*. Buckingham: Open University Press.

Youth Sport Trust (2000) *Towards Girl-Friendly Physical Education: Girls in Sport Partnership Project Final Report*. Loughborough: Institute of Youth Sport.

Index

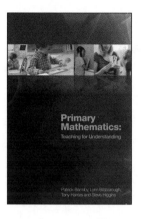

PRIMARY MATHEMATICS
Teaching for Understanding

Patrick Barmby, Lynn Bilsborough,
Tony Harries and Steve Higgins

9780335229260 (Paperback)
2009

eBook also available

This important book aims to support and develop teachers'
understanding of the key primary mathematics topics. By focusing on
understanding, the book draws attention to common misconceptions that
teachers may encounter in the classroom.

Key features:

- Specific focus on 'understanding' to offer new insights in to how to
  teach the topics
- Case studies to demonstrate how to communicate mathematical
  topics in the classroom
- End of chapter questions to stimulate discussion

The authors integrate research and theory throughout, to highlight core
issues. This theoretical background is also linked directly to classroom
practice and informs suggestions for how topics can be communicated
in the classroom

www.openup.co.uk

OPEN UNIVERSITY PRESS
McGraw - Hill Education

**EARLY CHILDHOOD AND
PRIMARY EDUCATION**
Readings and Reflections

Jane Johnston and John Halocha

9780335236565 (Paperback)
October 2010

This book explores the historical and philosophical ideas underpinning
practice in early childhood and primary education. It pulls together key
extracts from influential sources and provides helpful editorial
commentary explaining the importance of each article.

To help develop the necessary understandings and insights to engage in
critical debate on current issues in professional practice, this book
enables easy access to:

- Key theoretical ideas
- Reflective tasks
- Editorial commentary

www.openup.co.uk

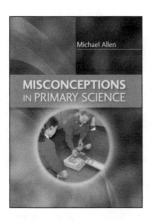

**MISCONCEPTIONS IN
PRIMARY SCIENCE**

Michael Allen

9780335235889 (Paperback)
February 2010

This essential book offers friendly support and practical advice for
dealing with the common misconceptions encountered in the primary
science classroom.

Most pupils will arrive at the science lesson with previously formed
ideas, based on prior reasoning or experience. However these ideas are
often founded on common misconceptions, which if left unexplained can
continue into adulthood.

This handy book offers 100 common misconceptions and advice for
teachers on how to recognise and correct such misconceptions.

Key features:

- Examples from the entire range of QCA Scheme of Work topics for
  Key Stages 1 and 2
- Practical strategies to improve pupils' learning
- Support for teachers who want to improve their own scientific
  subject knowledge

www.openup.co.uk

OPEN UNIVERSITY PRESS
McGraw · Hill Education